Literary Appreciation

Literary Appreciation

A practical guide to the understanding and enjoyment of literature in English

H. L. B. Moody

Longman

LONGMAN GROUP LTD
London
Associated companies, branches and representatives
throughout the world

© Longman Group Ltd 1968

All rights reserved. No part of this
publication may be reproduced, stored
in a retrieval system, or transmitted
in any form or by any means, electronic,
mechanical, photocopying, recording or
otherwise, without the prior permission
of the Copyright owner.

First published 1968
Seventh impression 1979

ISBN 0 582 60838 4

Printed in Singapore by
Kyodo-Shing Loong Printing Industries Pte Ltd.

To Bridget

Acknowledgements

I must first attribute the genesis of this book to Mallam Mohammed Awwal Ibrahim, whose poem *The Problem of Understanding Poetry*, written when he was a first-year student, originally gave me the idea of writing it. I am grateful for his permission to reprint it in this book (Appendix 1) although he himself has long ago, I believe, overcome the difficulties which it records.

I also wish to acknowledge encouragement and advice in the planning of the book given by Mr David Mallick, English Master at St Thomas' Secondary School, Kano; and, especially, by Mr F. O. Oridota, Senior English Master at Abeokuta Grammar School, Abeokuta, Western Nigeria – who would in fact have been a co-author had he not been whisked off for a year's British Council course in Edinburgh at a critical stage. I am grateful also to Mr Neil Bray, English Language Officer of the British Council, Kano, and to my publishers, for their discerning interest in this modest educational aid; and, last but not least, to Mr Ade Ojo, secretary of the English Department, Abdullahi Bayero College, Kano, for his devoted assistance as typist.

We are grateful to the following for permission to reproduce copyright material: (*The page numbers refer to Demonstration or Practice Passages given in this book*)

Author's agents for an extract from *Tell Freedom* (p. 173) by Peter Abrahams; The Bodley Head for an extract from *Ulysses* by James Joyce; the author for the poems 'Waiting' (p. 156) and 'Off the Campus' (p. 162) from *Sirens, Knuckles, Boots* by Dennis Brutus; Cambridge University Press for an extract from *Man and His Nature* (p. 111) by Charles Sherrington; to Jonathan Cape Ltd and the Hogarth Press for 'Newsreel' (p. 165) from *Collected Poems 1954* by Cecil Day Lewis; Chatto & Windus and Quentin Bell for an extract from *Civilization* (p. 175) by Clive Bell; Chatto & Windus and Mrs Laura Huxley for an extract from *Music at Night* (p. 142) by Aldous Huxley; Collins Publishers for an extract from 'The Miners' by Wilfred Owen; Curtis Brown Ltd for 'Zulu Girl' (p. 56) by Roy Campbell; J. M. Dent & Sons Ltd and the Trustees for the copyrights of the late Dylan Thomas for 'The Hand that Signed the Paper' (p. 160) from *Collected Poems* by Dylan Thomas; J. M. Dent & Sons Ltd and the Trustees of the Joseph Conrad Estate for an extract from *Typhoon* (p. 198) by Joseph Conrad; author's agents for 'A Polished Performance' (p. 98) from *Some Men Are Brothers* by D. J. Enright; Faber and Faber Ltd for 'Hawk Roosting' (p. 91) from *Lupercal* by Ted Hughes, for 'The Castle' (p. 161) from *Collected Poems* by Edwin Muir and for an extract from 'The Love Song of J. Alfred Prufrock', 'East Coker' and 'Charles Whibley' by T. S. Eliot; author's agents, Holt Rinehardt and Winston Inc. for 'A Considerable Speck' (p. 155) from *The Complete Poems* of Robert Frost; Rupert Hart-Davis Ltd for the poem 'A Peasant' (p. 154) by R. S. Thomas, from *The New Poetry*; the author for the poem 'Hornbills in Northern Nigeria' (p. 169) by John Heath-Stubbs; William Heinemann Ltd for an extract from *A Man of the People* (p. 105) by Chinua Achebe; Heinemann Educational Books Ltd for 'The Flute-Players' (p. 167) by J-J. Rabearivelo from *A Book of African Verse*, for an extract from 'And This, At Last' (p. 177) by John Nagenda and an extract from 'The Untilled Field' (p. 200) by Joseph Waiguru, both from *Origin East Africa* and for an extract from *The River Between* (p. 186) by James Ngugi; the author for his poem 'Me and the Animals' (p. 158) from *Imaginings* by David Holbrook; Hutchinson & Co (Publishers) Ltd for an extract from *Jagua Nana* (p. 181) by Cyprian Ekwensi and 'The Mountaineers' (p. 83) by Dannie Abse; Indiana University Press for 'You Tell me to Sit Quiet' (p. 170) by A. C. Jordan from *Poems from Black Africa*; the Executors of the James Joyce Estate and Jonathan Cape Ltd for an extract from *Portrait of the Artist as a Young Man* by James Joyce; author's agents and the Estate of the late Mrs Frieda Lawrence for an extract from *The Rainbow* (p. 133) and *The White Peacock* (p. 195) and for an extract from 'Song of a Man Who Has Come Through' from *The Complete Poems* by D. H. Lawrence; Longmans Green & Co Ltd for 'Fulani Cattle' (p. 153) and 'Segment VI from Ivbie: In the Cult of the Free' (p. 76) from *A Reed in the Tide* by J. P. Clark; Oxford University Press for extracts from 'The Windhover', 'The Wreck of the Deutschland' and 'Pied Beauty' from *The Poems of G. M. Hopkins*; Dr Lenrie Peters for his poem 'There I Lie' (p. 166); The Public Trustee and the Society of Authors for an extract from the Preface to *The Apple Cart* (p. 188) by G. B. Shaw; Routledge & Kegan Paul Ltd for extracts from *Practical Criticism* by Dr I. A. Richards; Sidgwick & Jackson Ltd for an extract from 'The Other Side of the Hedge' from *Collected Short Stories* by E. M. Forster; The Society of Authors as the literary representatives of the Estate of the late James Joyce for an extract from 'Gas From a Burner' by James Joyce; The Society of Authors as the literary representatives of the Estate of the late A. E. Housman and Messrs Jonathan Cape Ltd for an extract from 'A Shropshire Lad' by A. E. Housman, from *Collected Poems*; the author for 'Foruwa' (p. 119) by Efua T. Sutherland; Leonard Woolf and the Hogarth Press Ltd for an extract from *To the Lighthouse* (p. 184) by Virginia Woolf; author's agents, M. B. Yeats and Macmillan & Co Ltd for an extract from 'The Scholars' (p. 163) from *Collected Poems* by W. B. Yeats.

We have been unable to contact the copyright owners of the extract from 'This is Experience Speaking' (p. 179) by P. K. Buahin and the poem 'The Snowflakes' (p. 172) by Gabriel Okara.

Demonstration Passage no. 2 is by Thomas Carew; no. 4 by Percy Bysshe Shelley; no. 5 by Robinson Jeffers; no. 13 by Jonathan Swift. Practice Passage no. 5 is by Nicholas Tichborne; no. 7 by Matthew Arnold; no. 12 by Abraham Cowley; no. 27 by John Stuart Mill; no. 28 by Mark Twain; no. 30 by Matthew Arnold.

Contents

Foreword — xii

Introduction — 1
Two aims. The background. What is literature?
Why is literature important? Its value in education.
Discrimination. Judgement. The study of literature.
Practical Criticism. Criteria. Communication. Value.
Samples

Literary Appreciation in a second language — 9
Cultural differences. The complexity of English.
Connotations. Indirect Expression. Register.
Cultural references

Is it worth the effort? — 14
Reassurance

Method — 15

Comprehension — 16
Situation. Development. Intention

Technique — 19
Logical Structure. Choice of Words. Sound of Words.
Word Order. Rhythm. Rhyme. Figurative Language.
Simile and Metaphor. Personification. Symbolism. Irony.
Allusion. Form

Judgement — 38

Demonstrations

Poetry
 1 Love Song (Amharic) — 43

2	Ask Me No More	49
3	Zulu Girl	56
4	Ozymandias	63
5	The Eye	70
6	In the Cult of the Free	76
7	The Mountaineers	83
8	Hawk Roosting	91
9	A Polished Performance	98

Prose

10	Bori	105
11	The Eye	111
12	Foruwa	119
13	Utopia	126
14	The Cathedral	133
15	The Beauty Industry	142

Passages for practice

Poetry

1	Fulani Cattle	153
2	A Peasant	154
3	A Considerable Speck	155
4	Waiting (South African Style)	156
5	Elegy (on the night before his execution)	157
6	Me and the Animals	158
7	The Last Word	159
8	The Hand that Signed the Paper	160
9	The Castle	161
10	Off the Campus: Wits	162
11	The Scholars	163
12	Drinking	164
13	Newsreel	165
14	There I Lie	166
15	Flute-Players	167
16	Hornbills in Northern Nigeria	169
17	You Tell me to Sit Quiet	170
18	The Snowflakes	172

Prose

19	Festival	173
20	Civilization	175

21 Age and Youth	177
22 This is Experience Speaking	179
23 Electioneering	181
24 To the Lighthouse	184
25 Dilemma	186
26 Democracy	188
27 Heresy	191
28 The Balloon	193
29 Spring Funeral	195
30 The Blessing of Population	197
31 A Storm	198
32 Hoeing	200

Appendix I
The Problem of Understanding Poetry   203

Appendix II
Glossary and Index of Technical Terms   205

Foreword

This book has been planned for use by students taking
courses in higher education in parts of the world where
English is a Second Language.
It is extremely cumbersome continually to be using an
expression such as 'the student who uses English as
a Second Language', and this is abbreviated throughout
to 'the student'.
If any students whose first language is English
also find the book useful, we shall not be dismayed:
indeed, this will seem to bring closer together the
world-wide community of English-speaking peoples.

Introduction

TWO AIMS

This book has both a specific aim, and a more general aim. It has been produced, in the first place, to help students who are candidates in English for various Advanced Level or Higher Certificate Examinations (as, for example, that of the West African Examinations Council – or, as a part of the compulsory General Paper). It is even more specifically intended to help with the paper which calls for the appreciation of 'unseen' passages of verse and prose. But we do not in the least think of this as a mere 'cram' book, for its more general aim is to develop the art of literary appreciation, as the title indicates, and this cannot be done by any short-lived tricks (if indeed such things are ever really useful for examination candidates) but only by developing the powers of understanding, imagination and reflection, which is certainly part of any truly educational process. We do not altogether agree with the thesis of a book which has been recently published in England called *English versus Examinations* which implies that examinations in English are always hostile to the kinds of education which teachers of English aim at. If the teaching of English is concerned with the development of students' capacities of observation, memory, thought and feeling, examinations, and *preparation* for examinations, sensibly considered, can only call forth the best, most relevant response from students.

BACKGROUND

It is important for every student to have some background knowledge of the reasons for the inclusion of the 'appreciation' paper, and this will be found in the following pages, together with the outline of a method of procedure when dealing with unseen passages. No great originality is claimed for the theoretical part of this book, though an effort has been made to ensure that the essentials of this matter are clearly and helpfully set out. We do hope, however, that the practical applications of this book will be found useful, and give confidence in a field where at present much bewilderment prevails. In order to learn any technique, the student needs not only to learn the theory of that activity, but to practise it himself. Moreover, if he is to acquire any real proficiency in that technique, he must begin to practise it, as an apprentice, under the guidance of an expert, who will guide him through the early stages until he is able to take over for himself. Hence the three parts of this book:

EXPOSITION;
DEMONSTRATION;
PRACTICE.

Let us first consider the problem of 'literary appreciation' in its broadest aspects. Any intelligent student will wish to know how every one of his tasks fits into the general scheme of knowledge and education, and into each particular subject in the curriculum.

WHAT IS LITERATURE?

Literature springs from our inborn love of telling a story, of arranging words in pleasing patterns, of expressing in words some special aspect of our human experience. It is usually set down in printed characters for us to read, though some forms of it are performed on certain social occasions. There are a number of different branches such as Drama, Poetry, the Novel, the Short Story; all these are works of the imagination or the capacity for invention. The primary aim of literature is to give pleasure, to entertain those who voluntarily attend to it. There are, of course, many different ways of giving pleasure or entertainment, ranging from the most trivial and sensational to the most philosophical and profound. It is important to notice that the writer of literature is not tied to fact in quite the same way as the historian, the economist or the scientist, whose studies are absolutely based on what has actually happened, or on what actually does happen, in the world of reality.

WHY IS LITERATURE IMPORTANT?

We soon discover, however, that the literature which entertains us best does not keep us for long in the other-world of fantasy or unreality. The greatest pleasure and satisfaction to be found in literature occurs where (as it so often does) it brings us back to the realities of human situations, problems, feelings and relationships. The writers of literature, being less tied to fact than the historian or the scientist, have more scope to comment on the facts, to arrange them in unusual ways, and to speculate not only what *is*, but on what *ought to be*, or what *might be* (for better or worse). Writers are sometimes, therefore, people with visionary or prophetic insights into human life: Shelley wrote that poets are 'the unacknowledged legislators of the world'. In fact, with only a moderate knowledge of world history, we can easily acknowledge the vital part played in human affairs by writers. And all of us who read works of literature will find our knowledge of human affairs broadened and deepened, whether in the individual, the social, the racial or the international sphere; we shall understand the possibilities of human life, both for good and evil; we shall understand how we came to live at a particular time and place, with all its pleasures and vexations and problems; we shall understand the ways onwards which are open to us, and we shall perhaps be able to make right rather than wrong choices.

ITS VALUE IN EDUCATION

There is another value of an important kind which arises during the course of our education. Let us not underestimate the element of pleasure and enjoyment which comes from the reading of literature; this is surely in itself one of the great benefits which comes from being an educated person. But, over and above that, let us recognize that certain other fundamental skills and capacities are developed through the reading of literature, which are important to us all as educated people, not only in our private pleasures or our personal philosophies, but in the day-to-day exercise of the responsibilities which come to us in the modern world as a result of the educational qualifications we obtain. These skills include the capacities for discrimination, judgement and decision.

DISCRIMINATION

We have already said that the first motive for the reading of literature is pleasure or entertainment. True enough, but this is not the whole situation. Sooner or later, we begin to realize that we enjoy some things more than others, and that some of our reading experiences seem positively distasteful while others become more and more deeply absorbing. One way of explaining this would be to say that we are beginning to develop a taste for some things rather than for others. But this does not really go deep enough. What in fact is happening is that we are beginning to discriminate, to appreciate and feel the difference between what is really important, really first class, and what is trivial or easily dispensable. Human life is short, and human affairs are always moving on in ever increasing complexity: obviously the more surely we can give our attention to the important things rather than the trivial ones, the more we shall benefit, both in ourselves individually and in the contributions we shall be able to make to the world at large.

JUDGEMENT

As we continue to gain experience in discrimination, to compare our discrimination with other people's, particularly more experienced people; as we reflect upon our discriminations and discover on what factors they are based, we come towards a state of mind in which we feel a capacity for judgement; that is, for delivering an opinion about the rights and wrongs of a situation or a problem, which we find other people accept and agree to, which is not subsequently overturned, and which forms the best basis for many kinds of practical action. It is, indeed, quite realistic to suggest that the qualities developed in the thoughtful study of literature are of the greatest use in later years, for example to the employer who has to decide on the best applicant from amongst a number who have sent in written applications; to the publisher, who has to choose from amongst numerous manuscripts he receives those that are most worth publishing; and to the Minister, who has to weigh up the various courses of action which are recommended to him by his supporters, his leaders, possibly even by his opponents, and decide upon the best course of policy in the field of his particular responsibility.

THE STUDY OF LITERATURE

The previous paragraph may seem, to the student at the beginning of his Sixth Form course, to be looking impossibly far ahead into the future. We do not think so, however, and we are sure that the more realistically a student sets about his tasks in the Sixth Form, the better he will do them, the more he will enjoy them, the more he will see their significance, and the more effective a person he will become. We are not, in fact, claiming anything very new or revolutionary. In most of the great civilizations of the world, the training of the key members of the community has to a considerable extent been carried out through the medium of literary study, sometimes of the indigenous culture, sometimes (as in Renaissance Europe) that of another culture (i.e. the Greek and Roman Classics). There is no doubt, however, that in the latter part of the twentieth century, students of the literature written in the English language (which includes the literature of America and the Commonwealth) have an amply adequate body of material upon which a complete intellectual training can be based (especially if, in the later stages, an attempt is made to follow up some of the links which exist between literature in English and the literature of other cultures, European, African or Asian).

No educator who knows his way about the world of education would claim that the study of English literature is the *only* way by which we can train educated and effective members of the community. Undoubtedly all the other academic subjects or 'disciplines' can, if rightly taught and rightly studied, produce admirable results. Nevertheless, the study and appreciation of English literature offers special possibilities in a particularly convenient and concentrated way, and this brings us back to the specific aim of this book. We should like to give a brief account of the origin of, and the reasons behind, the kind of examination paper usually described as 'Passages of Verse and Prose for Appreciation'.

PRACTICAL CRITICISM

About thirty-five years ago, the field of English literary studies received an important new impetus. Until that time, training in literature had been very much based on what we should call 'comprehension' work, memory, exact translation and paraphrase, a a certain amount of analysis of character and motive, a certain amount of rather clumsy literary theorizing,[1] a certain amount of exchanging of literary opinions.[2] In 1929 there was published Dr. I. A. Richards' book *Practical Criticism*, which reported on some experiments he had carried out, and gave certain suggestions for teaching techniques, which have had a pronounced effect on English studies throughout the world. Dr Richards' 'experiments' have now developed into standard practice. He used to prepare anonymous extracts of poetry or poems, which he called protocols, and distribute them to his students who, without any hints or guidance from outside sources, had to digest, 'appreciate', and give their opinions on the 'protocols' week by week. After he had received the students' written opinions, he was able to analyze and compare them and make suggestions about his students' habits of reading and reasoning, and the way that these could be improved. Richards realized that, up to that time, an enormous part was played in literary studies by the generally accepted reputation of a writer, and that even 'those ... who have worthily occupied Chairs of Poetry (i.e. Professors) and taken their part in handing on the torch of tradition retrimmed, would probably admit in their secret souls that they have not read many poems with the care and attention that these anonymous items invite'.[3] By throwing his students entirely upon their own resources, he was aiming to bring out all their powers of observation, concentration, discrimination and judgement. He did not suggest that this was an easy matter, indeed the reverse: but the rewards were great.

> The critical reading of poetry is an arduous discipline; few exercises reveal to us more clearly the limitations under which, from moment to moment, we suffer. But, equally, the immense extension of our capacities that follows a

---

[1] One reads now, with a certain amazement such formulations as 'Poetry is a spirit' (Bradley); or 'Poetry is a continuous substance or energy whose progress is immortal' (Mackail).

[2] 'Give the plot of one or two of Crabbe's stories with any criticisms that may occur to you,' reads a question on an Honours Degree Examination in London in 1905.

[3] *Practical Criticism*, p. 316.

summoning of our resources is made plain. The lesson of
all criticism is that we have nothing to rely upon in making
our choices but ourselves.

These are the concluding words of his book, a book which should certainly be read by any teachers and students who are at all concerned with this study.

From the experiments which formed the basis of *Practical Criticism* the practice has gradually spread of asking students of English whether University Honours students, Sixth Formers, or even students at earlier stages in the educational pyramid, to pit themselves unaided against anonymous passages of verse and prose. This practice has been introduced into the system of examinations, but it has also been a feature of regular training. In Richards' book, it will be noted, his experiments were all centred on passages of poetry. Nowadays, the practice is usually extended to include passages of prose; and this seems entirely reasonable, for, as Wordsworth once said, 'There neither is, nor can be, any essential difference between the language of poetry and the language of prose.'

CRITERIA

We need to fill in the picture a little more before we can begin consideration of practical procedures. If we are to undertake a course involving discrimination and judgement, it is most helpful if we have some kind of criteria, or general principles, to guide us. And these are available. The theory used almost universally was formulated by I. A. Richards also, in his companion volume, *The Principles of Literary Criticism*. Until he wrote that book there was, as he put it, a 'chaos of critical theory'. He suggested that literature, as well as the other arts, can best be thought of as a process of *communication*, between the writer or the artist and his public, and this theory of communication has everywhere been found useful by writers and critics.

COMMUNICATION

With this idea at the back of our minds, we are in a position to judge any piece of writing, great or small. The test we apply is a double one:
1) Do we receive the impression that the particular poem or piece of prose effectively communicates what it sets out to do?

2) Is the idea (picture, character, or situation) communicated itself of any value to us?

Neither of these questions can be answered easily or automatically; each of them requires us to read carefully, reflect, and compare the impression received from one thing with those received from others. We need to know one further thing before we can make comparisons of 'value'.

VALUE

Richards supplied an answer to this question also, largely based on a psychological analysis of human character and the idea of what we call happiness. His answer, of course, followed the suggestions by some famous predecessors, as, for example, Coleridge, who said that the poet 'calls the whole soul of man into activity'. Richards' theory was, roughly, that the most valuable work of literature is the one which appeals to, satisfies and harmonizes the greatest number of human interests. This relates to the idea of an 'integrated personality' as opposed to the 'disturbed', 'maladjusted', or 'mixed-up' personality – which is becoming only too well known in the modern world. Among professional theorists there has been much discussion of this proposition, but we shall find it a useful way of distinguishing between *Macbeth* and *Sweeney Todd the Demon Barber*, or between Conrad's *The Secret Sharer* and Rider Haggard's *King Solomon's Mines*. It is not possible, in making comparisons of value, to be absolutely mathematical: but, with time and experience, one soon acquires some certainty, especially about the extremes of the scale. Some pieces of writing will seem skilful but trivial; others serious but clumsy; others both effective and penetrating, and so on. It is sometimes useful to supplement Richards' theory with a term coined by T. S. Eliot, the 'objective correlative', which signifies the verbal structure, standing independently by itself, as created by the writer, which must be sufficiently complete and self-explanatory to produce in the mind of the reader the conception which the author originally set out to convey.

SAMPLES

It may be objected at this point that we seem to have plunged into some confusion. The appreciation of literature is surely concerned with judgement of complete works: and the majority of works of literature are lengthy novels, plays, and poems. Yet the technique of judging we are studying at present seems concerned with either short poems, or short extracts of prose. Is there any connection between them? Yes. A very important one. When we are judging a lengthy work of literature, we shall certainly be concerned with some of its broader aspects, such as the unfolding of the plot, the development of the characters, the description of the setting and the background, the social problems presented, and so on. But, an equally important element in our judgement is our 'appreciation' of the 'texture' of the work. The metaphor of 'texture' invites comparison with the feel of the quality of a piece of cloth. It is in the *texture* of a larger work, in the actual interweaving and management of the very materials from which the work is constructed, i.e. the words used, that the best indication of its quality can nearly always be found. A writer's powers of observation and analysis; the integrity with which he handles his subject, and his sensitivity to words are indicated in quite small extracts. Experienced critics can sometimes tell with some certainty from just the first paragraph of a book whether it is a work of high quality, or just a routine, hackneyed piece of casual journalism. Thus, in training our powers of critical appreciation upon short pieces of writing (which are normally chosen, we presume, by teachers, textbook writers, and examiners who know what they are doing) we are developing an essential part of our equipment as students of literature. Understanding and recognition of the other elements of literary appreciation (analysis of plot, character, setting, theme etc.) do not really come within the scope of this book; and in any case, being more traditional, are better understood.

Literary Appreciation in a second language

The aim, the values, the techniques of literary appreciation sketched out here obviously originated in the country where English is the *first* language, and where every student will have had the English language in use for thousands of hours. Is it possible for the student who come to English as his second (possibly even third or fourth) language to manage the same feats of understanding and judgement? The answer is that, of course, he cannot manage them so quickly. Notable evidence of this is provided by the poem written by one of the author's students and reprinted as Appendix I. But, we should not suppose that this kind of work is easy even for native English speakers. Richards' experiments brought to light that many of the most expensively educated young English men and women of his day were quite hopeless, and absolutely bewildered *before they had received any special training*. However, where this training is available, through suitable books and well-trained teachers, few who have watched the progress of education in the emergent countries can doubt that students from these countries will increasingly be able to use and profit from such techniques, and that the whole community of English-speaking peoples throughout the world will as a result achieve closer and closer understanding of each other's mental processes and cultural experiences.

Nevertheless, this work is not easy, we recognize; there are special difficulties which we discuss briefly in the following paragraphs.

CULTURAL DIFFERENCES

In the 'older' countries of Europe, there has been developed a tradition of private reading and study, going back to the medieval monasteries, and, of course, greatly assisted by the development of printing, invented as far back as the fifteenth century. Nowadays in the countries of Europe and America, a tremendous outpouring of printed books comes from the publishers each year, and we can say that, broadly speaking, reading, whether of books, magazines or newspapers, is an established aptitude, even if the quality of reading-matter is not always high. This enables most people to read with a fair amount of ease and at a good speed. In the developing countries, which mostly lie in the tropical areas, circumstances have not, and still do not, favour reading as a habit. The shorter hours of daylight, absence of artificial light, lack of privacy, shortage of money, limited educational facilities, have all tended to limit opportunities for reading. In its place, of course, there has usually been a much more lively tradition of oral activity, conversation, greetings, oratory, story-telling, and discussion which has produced many excellent results, even if it has not favoured contact with the wide variety of minds and experiences which a written literature makes possible. In this respect, then, students using this book will usually have a less ready response to the written word. Again, from what we have seen of the enthusiasm for education, we expect this aptitude and sensitivity towards the written language to increase steadily in the future, especially where reading can be done under such circumstances as the use of this book implies.

THE COMPLEXITY OF ENGLISH

As we know, English has become the chief second language in many parts of the world, mainly for historical reasons; not because the English people have specially 'sold' it, and certainly not because it is a simple language. The English language has been in use for about six hundred years, and its resources have been continually developed by such things as contact with other cultures, the experiments and triumphs of great individual writers, the development of new social and scientific techniques, the controlling efforts of educationists and publishers, as well as the absolutely uncontrollable influence of the 'man in the street', until it has become exceptionally complex indeed. Students obviously should begin by learning the simplest and most basic forms of the language, and will often be held up and puzzled by some of the less standard forms of expression, whether these are of the most ornate and artificial:

> Much have I travelled in the realms of gold
> And many goodly states and kingdoms seen ...
> (when the author, Keats, is talking of the great books he has read),

or of the most terse and colloquial:
> Now, shut up, clear out, and beat it!

CONNOTATIONS

We know, too, that when any language has been in use for a long time, many of its words and expressions acquire a peculiar richness of significance. We talk about the 'denotation' of a word, which is its primary meaning, as defined in any dictionary, and the 'connotations', which are all the additional 'flavours' and 'associations' which it carries. Poets particularly often depend a great deal on this characteristic of language, and obviously students whose acquaintance with a language has been limited will not automatically be able to get the feeling of this richness: the more they can read and build up their experience, the more fully will they become sensitive to it.

INDIRECT EXPRESSION

Only a few English writers have consistently used the simplest forms of the language; even some of those who have claimed to have not always kept to their policy. We must remember, indeed, that most writers have not been writing for schoolboys, schoolgirls, or students (even of their own mother-tongue). They have been writing to please, to interest, to sell their works to the book-reading public of their own day. And, as we know with other matters involving personal taste, such as clothing, people all over the world have not been content with the simplest way of doing things, but have tried to express their individuality by ingenuity, magnificence, originality, colour, extravagance, even sometimes by puzzling or startling the public. As a special aspect of this, we know that many poets using the English language during the last fifty years have quite deliberately made their poetry difficult or 'obscure', partly for fear of being too commonplace. It is to be hoped that students will not be asked, too early, to understand or appreciate some of the more extravagant flights of fancy which have been used in the course of English literature. But they must be ready to see the point of some of the methods of indirect expression which they will encounter, such as metaphor, simile, irony, and we know that in practice they can do this, for usually their own language possesses similar features.

REGISTER

Another aspect of the English language which may cause additional problems when it comes to the appreciation of literature is 'register', a matter which is becoming discussed a good deal nowadays. The English language has resources which enable us to express thoughts in a number of different ways, according to the occasion; just as a person may have one outfit of clothes for work; another for sport;

another for dancing; another for going to church, and another for ceremonial occasions.

These words spoken by Mr Casaubon in George Eliot's *Middlemarch* indicate that the speaker is a rather pedantic, pompous person:
> The task, notwithstanding the assistance of my amanuensis, has been a somewhat laborious one, but your society has happily prevented me from that too continuous prosecution of thought beyond the hours of study which has been the snare of my solitary life.

A more direct and sincere way of saying the same might be:
> Even with your help, the work of writing has been hard, but your company has prevented me from overworking as I often used to do before we were married.

A correct understanding of register is obviously important in the practical use of English, in letter-writing, and in approaching different kinds of people. Similarly, in order to get the correct impression in literary appreciation, it is necessary to be sensitive to various kinds of register, and sometimes of changes in register.

CULTURAL REFERENCES

We shall often be aware that the literature written in the English language has been written against the background of English history, social customs, climate, geography, flora and fauna, which differ considerably from those in other parts of the world; and that many common expressions (e.g. *slave, sea, snow, wood, rose, love*) do not necessarily have the same meaning in other parts of the world that they do in England. This difficulty may cause some slowing-up or uncertainty in the appreciation of English literature. Nevertheless, we should not make too much of this difficulty: it is a characteristic of an educated person to be open-minded and to have an imaginative curiosity about the circumstances of life in other parts of the world, and no English readers, I think, will reasonably complain about difficulty in understanding such things as *palms, lagoons, deserts, camels, igloos, kraals*, although these do not occur in the British Isles.

Is it worth the effort?

REASSURANCE

In the six previous paragraphs, we have described briefly some of the obstacles which come between the student and the successful appreciation of English literature; and before we go any further we ought to face the question: in view of the difficulties, is it worth the effort? In the modern world, so full of urgent problems, is it worth persevering with the task of introducing students to the appreciation of English literature? Would it not be better to concentrate on the appreciation and development of literature in the various indigenous languages? Would it not be better to concentrate on learning the English language in its simplest forms for commercial or scientific purposes, and discard all the 'complications' to be found in the study of literature? Is the desire to know something of English literature just one of those vain and superfluous 'prestige' ambitions, which has no longer any relevance for politically independent nations?

Some students, and some teachers, without giving much serious thought to the problem, will no doubt answer 'Yes'. The author of this book is convinced that the answer must be 'No'. As long as a sensible selection and grading is observed, students *can, should* and *will* enter fully into the riches which the art of literary appreciation will unlock. And this view is based not on wishful thinking, but on the undeniable fact that throughout the far-flung areas of the English-speaking world, there are large numbers of educated people who know, beyond any matter of self-deception, that they have *enjoyed* a great deal of the literature that they have read and studied, and that much of it has been deeply meaningful and helpful in their own lives. For evidence, we may read William Conton's account of his debt in *The African*; and we may observe how *Things Fall Apart* and *No Longer at Ease*, two of the most notable novels to be written recently in the Commonwealth, have taken their very apt titles from English poems (*The Second Coming*, by W. B. Yeats, and *The Journey of the Magi*, by T. S. Eliot).

Method

In the following sections we set out a method of approach which will be useful both in examination work, and more generally in the field of literary appreciation. At first it will be advisable for the student to work carefully through the various stages suggested. When he becomes more experienced he will forget about this 'method', and function much more spontaneously. Nevertheless there is a definite logic in the method of procedure adopted, and it will always be useful.

An important part in the plan of this book is to make little distinction between prose and poetry. It is, of course, possible to make distinctions between prose and poetry in the abstract, but when it comes to making an appreciation of either form, we suggest that it is best to apply the same tests. There are good theoretical grounds for this. Both poetry and prose are regarded as forms of communication; and, in fact, the more we look into the matter, the more we find that the forms of expression we may be inclined to expect chiefly in poetry, also often occur in prose, and that many of the less spectacular qualities of prose also play an important part in any poem. It is essential that we should approach any task of appreciation with an open and an observant mind; and not to assume that because *this* piece looks like a poem, only certain types of expression or idea can be found in it, or because *that* piece of writing is set out as prose, it can contain nothing of the more poetic elements in it. We have already seen Wordsworth's saying that 'there neither is, nor can be, any essential difference between the language of poetry and the language of prose'. And I. A. Richards stresses the same point when he reminds us that one of the chief obstacles to a proper appreciation of poetry is the failure 'to make out its *prose* sense, its plain, overt meaning, as a set of ordinary intelligible English sentences, taken quite apart from any further poetic significance'.[1]

If we do seek to elaborate the distinction between prose and poetry, we shall probably come to the oft-repeated conclusion that poetry is often a more complex form of expression, calling on more of the resources of language than prose usually does. For the purposes of this book, and the method of appreciation we recommend,

---
[1] *Practical Criticism*, p. 13.

we shall minimize the distinction because there are so many exceptions to it. How often, for example, are various kinds of rhythm and metaphor found in prose, and how important always in a poem is the element of clarity of thought!

Comprehension

This is the first essential stage in appreciation: and no kind of appreciation is possible unless there has first been comprehension. Indeed full and accurate comprehension will often take us a long way into any piece of writing. Since this stage is vital, it is important not to be hasty with it. Read your passage over and over again, until you are satisfied that you are getting the right sense. If you are feeling rather nervous, if for example, you are in an examination room, you can get a grip on the situation by reading the passage to yourself, in a whisper. (You may have been taught normally not to 'vocalize' your reading – but this is a special occasion.) The act of reading the passage physically will compel you to attend to the words one by one in the correct order, which will be of great help in building up its basic meaning. Don't try to ask yourself questions such as 'Am I enjoying this? Why do I enjoy this?' You are probably not enjoying it at all, at this stage. Don't ask yourself 'What am I feeling about this? What emotion is it arousing?' Concentrate entirely on grasping the situation which the passage presents. Don't be alarmed if this stage takes some time. Remember that you are using your mind to bring fully into your thoughts something of which there was no trace previously. Compare yourself, if you like, to the pilot of an aeroplane crossing the desert, of a ship crossing the ocean: suddenly, in the midst of the empty spaces, he is aware of an unfamiliar object; he wonders what it is, he goes closer, eagerly looking for any signs which tell him more exactly what it is he is looking at: every little detail he can observe, possibly a flag, a trace of smoke, a slight movement may help to give him an idea. As he gets closer and closer he sees other details which help him to confirm or reject his first thoughts, until at length he is close enough, all his observations confirm each other and he sees exactly what it is, a broken-down trans-Saharan bus, or perhaps an American satellite which has come down at an unexpected place in the Atlantic ocean!

Do allow your efforts at comprehension to be very much guided by the grammatical structure of the passage you are looking at. If you merely pick out certain nouns, for example, and jump to a conclusion by stringing them together, you may easily go wrong. Look for the main verbs in each sentence; notice which nouns are the subjects of the verbs; notice how these main parts of the sentence are modified by other words and clauses; notice how one sentence is set in relation to the next, whether in continuation or in contrast, and so on.

SITUATION

The results of your efforts in comprehension should leave you with a feeling of having grasped something. You will, we hope, have managed to see the passage as a report on a situation, or possibly as a picture. Often the situation will consist of a person (young? old? boy? girl? man? woman? farmer? student? airman? etc. etc.) at a recognizable place, and at a specific time. It may be concerned not with one person, but a group. And, in this situation, he or they will be concerned with something; waiting for something; trying to do something; discussing something. In fact it is the old pair of Subject and Predicate in a more extended form. If you have looked at the evidence carefully, you may have discovered that there are other people, or things, concerned in this situation: a man may be thinking about a woman, a boy may be thinking about his father: a farmer may be thinking about his harvest: a statesman may be thinking about his country: a reverent person may be thinking about his God. It is impossible to suggest all the possibilities; here we are just illustrating the kind of situation which you will find, and must grasp, before you go any further.

It is necessary to remember that the situation presented in a poem may not always be a real one, something actually observed in reality. Since poets are gifted with imagination, we must be ready to adjust our thoughts and our feelings to 'situations' which are based perhaps on hypothesis, or fantasy, which may never actually have happened, which perhaps never could happen, or in which certain ex. elements of fantasy mingle with aspects of reality. For example, T. S. Eliot's poem *The Journey of the Magi* (probably already well known to students using this book) expresses the memories and reflections of one of the three Wise Kings who travelled to Palestine some two thousand years ago for the birth of the new Messiah, Jesus: the poet tries to imagine these reflections as they might have occurred in the mind of the King at the very end of his life, years after his historic journey. The poem is based on no known historical facts or documents: it is entirely an invention of the poet's imagination; yet how self-consistent and meaningful it becomes when we have worked it out. As another example of a different kind, Wilfred Owen's poem *Futility* refers to a young soldier who has been killed in a battle during the First World War, and the poem takes the form of a speculation (quite unrealistic, and quite unscientific) as to whether, since the sun is the great source of life, the soldier might come to life again if he were moved into the sunshine. This speculation, comparing various aspects of life and death, forms the basis of a deep moving poem mourning for the lives cut tragically short in war.

Thus, in seeking to identify and clarify the 'situation' in a given poem or passage, our minds must be as flexible and alert as possible: ready to grasp the situation not only in general terms but in its precise details.

DEVELOPMENT

It may be that the situation you discover in a piece of writing is entirely static, i.e. nothing in it moves, or changes, or develops. This might be true, for example, of a piece of scenic description. Usually, however, there will be some kind of development or movement indicated in the passage. Sometimes this will be a physical movement of some kind (as of a labourer going home after a day's work). Very often the development will be in the nature of some thoughts or reflections which arise, and follow one another, as the writer looks upon a certain scene, or contemplates a certain problem (as for example, a writer hearing the song of a bird and describing the series of thoughts and feelings which pass through his mind as a consequence). It is very important to perceive how a piece of writing begins, how it develops and how it ends, and this contributes a great deal to the subject of our next paragraph. Do not, of course, expect that situation and development will always be neatly set out: at times it will be necessary to infer these from passing hints or suggestions.

INTENTION

By now, having spent a good deal of time clarifying the situation and its development, you may quite easily be able to indicate what the writer's main *intention*, or purpose, was in writing the passage. Was it, for example, to give a clear explanation of how to do something; to give a detailed impression of life in a certain city; to explain the motives behind a person's actions; to ridicule something which is unworthy or undesirable; to share with us certain very precious feelings; to cause us to admire something beautiful; to evoke pity for someone in unfortunate circumstances? In terms such as these, or sometimes much more extended terms if the intention is not quite so simple, we can explain to ourselves that we have caught the writer's aim. If we feel some certainty about this, it is perhaps some evidence that the writer's communication has been successful.

Technique

> POLONIUS: '*What do you read, my Lord?*'
> HAMLET: '*Words, words, words.*'

The first general stage of appreciation which we have been writing about so far is largely spontaneous. That is to say, we just read and re-read the chosen piece of material with an open, a receptive mind, and know that factors such as our observation, our vocabulary, our power 'to put two and two together', and the writer's skill in his choice and arrangement of language, together with all our accumulated experience of reading, thinking, and acting – all these will re-create in our mind, and communicate to us, a great deal of what the writer intended to convey to us.

The second stage of appreciation is more deliberate; more concerned with analysis. At this stage we attempt to gain a conscious understanding of the means by which the writer's effect is conveyed.

This is in accordance with the very natural instinct of the human mind – the desire to discover causes; and is found in all branches of human activity, as for example, the historian who seeks to discover not only *what* happened at a particular time and place, but *why* it happened; or the doctor who is not only curious to discover whether a person is alive or dead, but will try to find out the *causes* of death, or at least the nature of the disease. Most people know the classic story of Sir Alexander Fleming who puzzled out the *causes* of the death of some of his cultivated bacteria until he made the discovery of penicillin.

Most students at first find this analysis of a writer's means difficult. Others will say that it destroys the enjoyment of any piece of writing, and this school of thought is often summed up in Wordsworth's famous line:

> We murder to dissect.

The experiences of most intelligent people, however, is that analysis does not spoil enjoyment – rather the reverse. The more we understand exactly how any human achievement has been brought about, from the writing of a poem, the climbing of a mountain, the running of a mile in four minutes, to the building of a dam, or a new nation, the more our appreciation of human life will be extended and deepened.

In the following pages we suggest a method of approach to the analysis of literary technique.

LOGICAL STRUCTURE

In the appreciation of any piece of writing, whether serious or light-hearted, poetry or prose, the first thing we must attend to is the basic, logical, foundation of sense, or meaning. This we grasp by following out in our minds the construction of each sentence; detecting what it is telling us about (i.e. what is its 'subject'), and what is said (or 'predicated') of it. Yes, even poetry is basically constructed of analyzable sentences, although the words may be spaced out in a special way on the page. It is next important to be aware of the relationship between the parts of each sentence; and to be clear, for example, in reading a complex sentence, which is the principal idea (or 'clause') and in what various ways the subsidiary clauses are used to amplify or limit it. Next it is important to observe how sentence is related to sentence; whether in the form of the continuation of a train of thought or explanation; whether by setting one statement in sharp contrast with its predecessor; whether by assembling a number of parallel statements which all lead to a certain conclusion; whether by introducing a general idea, and then deducing a number of results which follow from it. The possible variations of thought are more than we can classify, but it is essential in the first stage of 'appreciation' to carry out this stage with all the powers of thought and concentration that we can provide.

Although we have been assuming that there will usually be a logical structure in any passage of writing, there may, of course, be occasions when, for special purposes, the structure is contrary to logic. Shakespeare, for example, expresses Hamlet's emotional disturbance by giving him words to speak in which the logical thread is severely broken:

> ... Why she would hang on him
> As if increase of appetite had grown
> By what it fed on and yet, within a month!
> Let me not think on't. Frailty thy name is woman!
> A little month, or ere those shoes were old
> With which she followed my poor father's body ...

And in the following passage from *Ulysses*, James Joyce seems to ignore the usual kind of logical sequence in order to convey the drift of sensations through Molly Bloom's mind as she lies in bed unable to get to sleep:

> ... a quarter after what an unearthly hour I suppose they're just getting up in China now combing out their pigtails for the day well soon have the nuns ringing the angelus they've nobody coming in to spoil their sleep except an odd priest or two for his night office the alarm clock next door at cockshout clattering the brains out of itself let me see if I doze off 1 2 3 4 5 what kind of flowers are those they invented like the stars the wall paper in Lombard Street was much nicer the apron he gave me was like that something only I only wore it twice better lower this lamp and try again so as I can get up early ...

Again in some other kinds of writing the principle of logic may have been set aside, in order to gain a more life-like effect.

Even when a passage is fundamentally logical, we should not expect it always to be quite simple. We should recognize that, to both writers and readers, a considerable amount of aesthetic pleasure comes from the clever or startling use of the intellect, and that often quite simple thoughts can be decked out in the most surprising and elaborate ways. Without at first correctly comprehending this logical structure of the passage under consideration, it is almost pointless to go on to search for other elements or beauties, for everything will be out of focus. Richards in *Practical Criticism* attributed much of the failure to make a correct appreciation of the 'protocols' to just this 'widespread inability to construe meaning'.

If we have concentrated on discovering the basic 'prose' meaning of any passage, we shall be safeguarded against going too far wrong in our appreciation. Furthermore, in reading and re-reading to trace out the basic meaning, many of the other elements of language will, without our realizing it, have been making their impression upon us. Having firmly grasped the basic meaning, our next object will be to consider the kind of impact or impression the passage makes upon us; the particular colour or flavour which the writer has aimed to impart to his subject.

It will be noticed incidentally that in this book we have avoided using the word Style in connection with literary appreciation – although it is often used when discussing literature. Of course 'style' – a manner of doing something (for example, a style of dress, a style of hairdressing, a style of running) is commonly used in many connections. We avoid it in this book because we wish to encourage students to go beyond the simple concept of Style, and to analyze more exactly the factors which contribute to the effect of any piece of writing – on the lines suggested in the following sections.

CHOICE OF WORDS

The words which, over and above the basic meaning, carry the real flavour of a piece of writing are usually the Verbs, the Adjectives, and to some extent the Adverbs, and it is very well worth while to look at these carefully. The English language, we know, is very rich in alternatives, and it is well to ask ourselves in considering each of these just why it is 'so and not otherwise'. Sometimes it is useful to consider what alternatives could have been used, and whether any of them would have been more suitable. Then we can begin to value the effect of the one that the writer has actually used. For example, Shakespeare gives his impression of woods in autumn, the melancholy season when all the leaves fall off the trees in deciduous forests, as

> 'Bare ruined *choirs* where late the sweet birds sang.'

If we try out various alternatives to 'choirs' (e.g. woods, towers, glades, roads, scenes, shades) we find that none of them give the impression of abandoned musical cathedral-like majesty that Shakespeare's actual choice does. Again, in Coleridge's vision of the palace of 'Kubla Khan', the description of the woman 'wailing' for her demon lover is better than if she had been described as 'screaming'. A woman screams on quite ordinary, sometimes ridiculous occasions, and a scream, though loud, is of definite duration and soon over, whereas 'wailing' suggests a much more prolonged and mournful, even supernatural effect.

At this stage we shall obviously be recalling what was said on page 11 about the association of words. We shall remember, too, that even words which are fairly close together in meaning have different 'associations', based largely on the way they have been used by generations of bygone writers; in fact, that 'there *are* no synonyms'. So, we shall try to discover why the writer has decided to use just *those* words rather than others, and in thinking about this question we shall find out a good deal about the effect he is trying to produce. For example, at the end of a short story by E. M. Forster called *The Other Side of the Hedge*, the narrator is falling asleep in a very beautiful landscape:

> Though my senses were sinking into oblivion, they seemed to expand ere they reached it. They perceived the magic song of nightingales, and the odour of invisible hay, and stars piercing the fading sky ...

We could discuss some of the words chosen here and consider why the author has chosen to use *song*, instead of chant, air, ballad, music, tune, warbling or twittering;

odour, instead of smell, scent, perfume, stink, aroma or stench;

piercing, instead of penetrating, stabbing, holing, dotting, decorating or ornamenting.

The choice of words is also a very good indication of the register of a passage; and from a careful consideration of the words chosen, in contrast to other similar ones which were not chosen, we can tell whether the writer intended it to be dignified or colloquial; mocking or serious; earnest or flippant, and so on.

SOUNDS OF WORDS

Words, although chiefly symbols, are nevertheless (especially in their spoken form) sounds; and we know that it is possible to select words which, as individual sounds and in the patterns which they can be made to form, can have a special effect in underlining, emphasizing, imitating or suggesting the writer's meaning. It is well known, too, how words can be selected to intensify the impression of horses galloping, water falling, rivers flowing, soldiers marching, birds flying, the moon rising and so on. What special 'sound effects', for example, are achieved in these three extracts?

> The lights begin to twinkle from the rocks
> The long day wanes: the slow moon climbs: the deep
> Moans round with many voices.
>
> Tennyson: *Ulysses*

> Listen! you hear the grating roar
> Of pebbles which the waves draw back, and fling
> At their return, up the high strand,
> Begin, and cease, and then again begin
> With tremulous cadence slow, and bring
> The eternal note of sadness in.
>
> Arnold: *Dover Beach*

> High there, how he rung upon the rein of a wimpling wing
> In his ecstasy! then off, off forth on swing,
> As a skate's heel sweeps smooth on a bow-bend.
>
> G. M. Hopkins: *The Windhover*

Another aspect of the sound of words is that described by the terms 'alliteration' and 'assonance', patterns of sound repetition, respectively of consonants or vowels. These devices are not often used deliberately to create specific effect, but are often found in passages of prose or verse which convey a special emotional power. It is possible that this is seen in many languages, for the mind when undergoing strong excitement often seems to express itself in some rhythmic form. For example, the poetry of the Anglo-Saxons used alliteration as its chief rhythmic device, and students familiar with other languages, whether European or African, can find examples in plenty outside English altogether. One of the chief effects of alliteration seems to be to bind words together in a kind of close, significant relationship, the *exact* significance of which, of course, is given to us by the sense of the words. Here, for example, is a stanza from G. M. Hopkins' poem *The Wreck of the Deutschland*, a ship which was wrecked on a sandbank in the North Sea. Notice the use of alliteration (as well as rhythm) in suggesting the violent confusion, as the ship is repeatedly buffeted in the stormy sea:

> She drove in the dark to leeward
> She struck, not a reef or a rock
> But the combs of a smother of sand, night drew her
> Dead to the Kentish Knock;
> And she beat the bank down with her bows and the ride
> of her keel:
> The breakers rolled on her beam with ruinous shock,
> And canvas and compass, the whorl and the wheel
> Idle for ever to waft her or wind her wick, these she
> endured.

WORD ORDER

We probably remember without any difficulty that there is a 'word order' which is normal to the English language: it is often shown in language-teaching books in such codes as:

S. V. O.
S. V. O. D.O.

There is + Noun + Infinitive
etc., etc.

The more familiar we are with the language, in either spoken or written form, the more our minds will unconsciously expect one or other of the normal patterns to be present. Imaginative writers, however, in order to give special prominence to some aspects of their writing, are found to change the normal order in various ways. The opening of A. E. Housman's poem *Easter*:

> Loveliest of trees, the cherry now
> Is hung with bloom along the bough ...

is much more dramatic and rhythmic than if the words followed the normal prose order (i.e. 'the cherry, loveliest of trees, is now hung with bloom along the bough'). One of the most striking uses of the disruption of normal word order is found in Hopkins' poem *Pied Beauty*, in praise of the marvellous diversity of the created universe:

> All things counter, original, spare, strange;
> Whatever is fickle, freckled (who knows how?)
> With swift, slow; sweet, sour; adazzle, dim;
> He fathers forth whose beauty is past change ...

The Subject here is 'He' (God) in the fourth line; the Verb is 'fathers forth', and once we have noted these, we see that the first three lines are the rather complex Object of the sentence. The inversion of sentence order here seems to symbolize the way in which we may for a long time be fascinated by the diversity of creation, and it is only after some time that we discover that God is the author of it all. Since 'He' (God) emerges at the end of the list of his varied creations, the short clause defining his eternal changelessness (Whose beauty is past change) comes with powerful final effect.

Students will undoubtedly come across other examples which may at first cause some uncertainty. Nevertheless, it will be observed that normal word order especially in modern English poetry is very much more common.

RHYTHM

Alliteration, the repetition of similar consonantal sounds, leads us on to the topic of rhythm, a very important aspect of language. Rhythm, whether we use the word to apply to words, music, drumming; to wave motion, landscape, or even architecture or mathematics, is fundamentally a matter of the repetition of patterns – repetition accompanied by a certain amount of development and variation. An appreciation of rhythm is embedded deeply in human consciousness, and no doubt derives from such basic physical processes as breathing, eating, the succession of day and night, or the seasons. Both poetry and prose make extensive use of rhythm, though the effect is often more easy to recognize and describe in poetry than in prose.

It is necessary to distinguish between Rhythm and Metre (and their attendant science of Scansion). In earlier centuries, literary enthusiasts tried to impose upon English the terminology which had been used to describe Classical poetry, with such things as metrical 'feet', Iambs, Trochees, Dactyls, Anapaests, Spondees and so on. While this may have had a certain amount of interest and use, it probably did more harm than good. It is true that in many kinds of writing and speech there is an underlying pattern of stressed and unstressed syllables (and in English poetry we can say that the Iambic foot is almost everywhere prevalent), but it is a great fallacy to suppose that all words in English poetry are *either* stressed *or* unstressed. In fact, any piece of writing involves many subtle differences of rhythmic stress, and it is far more important to be able to recognize their relation to the topic of a passage than to be able to 'pick them out' in isolation. The correct relation between metre and rhythm can be expressed by saying that many pieces of writing are based upon a fundamental metre or 'measure', but the important thing to concentrate on is the rhythmic effects which are imposed upon the metre. We should consider the analogy of a Jazz group which has its so-called 'rhythm section', pounding out tirelessly and endlessly a basic unvaried pattern of sound, while superimposed on this is the 'melody section', which usually seems to be performing many agile and spectacular improvisations upon the bass provided by the others. Without the 'melody', the 'rhythm' section would be of very little interest.

Thus in appreciating a piece of literature our aim will be not to describe basic metrical patterns, but to notice and to point out how certain words, or certain features of the passage, are given special prominence by the rhythm, in relation to the main aim of the passage.

Thus in the stanza already quoted from *The Wreck of the Deutschland* (page 25), it is important to note *not* that line 5 is composed of five anapaestic feet but that the strongly accentuated rhythm here gives a vivid impression of a storm-driven ship battering itself to pieces against the sandbank.

A different kind of rhythm effect is seen in T. S. Eliot's lines from the *Love Song of J. Alfred Prufrock*:

> For I have known them all already, known them all –
> Have known the evenings, mornings, afternoons.
> I have measured out my life with coffee spoons.

Here the three-fold repetition of 'known' gives the impression of exasperated weariness with cosmopolitan life which the writer seeks to convey.

RHYME

This is the patterned repetition of similar-sounding word-endings, usually at the ends of lines of verse, and it is in fact a special aspect of Rhythm. It is easy to recognize, and many students love to set out rhyme patterns in algebraic symbols
    a, b; a, b: c, d, e; c, d, e ...
The important thing however is to be able to recognize and explain the effect with which rhyme is being used. Sometimes it is to add emphasis to an important statement,

> For thy sweet love remembered such wealth brings
> That then I scorn to change my state with Kings.
>
> Shakespeare: *Sonnet XXV*

Sometimes, especially if intensified by double rhymes (i.e. correspondence of the two final syllables) it has a humorous, or satirical effect,

> Ladies and gents, you are here assembled
> To hear why earth and heaven trembled
> Because of the black and sinister arts
> Of an Irish writer in foreign parts.
>
> Joyce: *Gas from a Burner*

Sometimes it intensifies the melodious effect of pieces of writing
which deal with lyrical, musical, or pleasurable subjects,

> There is sweet music here that softer falls
> Than petals from blown roses on the grass,
> Or night dews on still waters between walls
> Of shadowy granite, in a gleaming pass;
> Music that gentler on the spirit lies
> Than tired eyelids upon tired eyes.
>
> Tennyson: *The Lotos Eaters*

During the present century, some poets have made interesting use of
half-rhymes, in which the correspondence of sounds is only partly
complete:

> There was a whispering in my hearth, [h a:θ]
>   A sigh of the coal, [koul]
> Grown wistful of a former earth [ə:θ]
>   It might recall. [rikɔ:l]
>
> Wilfred Owen: *The Miners*

FIGURATIVE LANGUAGE

We normally use language 'literally', i.e. according to its generally
agreed primary sense; we also sometimes use it 'figuratively', i.e.
in various indirect ways, which are sometimes called Figures of
Speech. Again the ancient writers of handbooks on the art of
Rhetoric (the art of persuasion) managed to classify and name these,
and some modern textbooks still preserve the whole range of these
'figures', with such names as Oxymoron, Litotes, Synecdoche,
Hypallage, Zeugma and so on. It is true that all these figures, which
were originally detected and described in the older classical European languages, can be found and illustrated in English literature, if
we look hard enough. However, we must keep a sense of proportion
and a sense of relevance, and in this book we shall not use more
of these than seem to be really necessary in our main purpose of
increasing literary appreciation.

SIMILE AND METAPHOR

These are two linguistic devices, both involving the use of comparison, which will often be met. When anyone, private citizen or professional writer, is trying to explain an idea with particular exactness or force, he may often find the more obvious supply of words insufficiently exact, or insufficiently exciting, and he will often strive for a bolder impression by making a comparison with some other branch of his knowledge or experience. Thus an unhappy lover can compare his tormented feelings to *fire*; a student can *grapple* with a difficult problem; we can speak of a man as of *sterling* quality (at the time of writing sterling is still one of the world's reliable currencies!); some pages back, in more colloquial speech, we spoke of a maladjusted person as 'mixed-up'. The use of comparison runs throughout the history of language, and has produced some of the most beautiful descriptive writing in the English language. The Simile, of course, opens with a clear recognition of the comparison: Romeo speaks of the amazing beauty of Juliet

> O she doth teach the torches to burn bright,
> It seems she hangs upon the cheek of night
> *Like* a rich jewel in an Ethiop's ear.

J. P. Clark describes a famous African city thus:
> Ibadan,
>   running splash of rust
> and gold – flung and scattered
> among seven hills, *like* broken
> china in the sun.

D. H. Lawrence writes of his longing to change some of the moribund ideas of his contemporaries:

> If only, most lovely of all, I yield myself and am borrowed
> By the fine, fine wind that takes its course through
>   the chaos of the world
> *Like* a fine, and exquisite chisel, a wedge-blade inserted;
> If only I am keen and hard *like* the sheer tip of a wedge
> Driven by invisible blows,

> The rock will split, we shall come at the wonder, we shall
> find the Hesperides.

Metaphor is in a sense more unconscious than simile and is deeply embedded in the choice of words, controlled by the predominant idea. Hamlet is disgusted with the corrupt world he has discovered:

> How weary, flat, stale and unprofitable
> Seem to me all the uses of this world.
> Fie on't! ah fie! 'Tis an unweeded *garden*
> That grows to seed ...

T. E. Hulme puts the following metaphor into the mouth of a 'fallen gentleman' who has no house to sleep in:

> O God make small
> The old star-eaten *blanket* of the sky
> That I may fold it round me and in comfort lie.

T. S. Eliot, despairing of ever being able to express his thoughts and feelings, writes thus, at a certain point in *East Coker*:

> That was a way of putting it – not very satisfactory
> Leaving one still with the intolerable *wrestle*
> With words and meanings.

We should note that comparisons of either of these kinds may be either very brief and refer only to a relatively small detail, or they may be sustained for a considerable time, sometimes throughout a whole passage or poem. Sometimes, as the examples in this section illustrate, similes and metaphors come tumbling out of the poet's mind in profusion, as when J. P. Clark thinks of Ibadan first as something *splashed* out, and then *like* pieces of 'broken china'.

A term which has been used to excess in recent years in literary appreciation is the word 'imagery'. We have resolved to abandon the use of this word, because there seems no clear agreement as to whether it is applied to metaphor and simile or to picturesque descriptive writing of a literal kind. It has been a very fashionable word, but we can say everything we have to say more exactly without it.

Sometimes we find it useful to employ the word 'conceit', with the special meaning given to it by poets of the sixteenth and seventeenth century, to signify an extremely original and unexpected metaphor e.g.

> 'The fringed *curtains* of thine eye advance'
>
> Shakespeare: *The Tempest*

PERSONIFICATION

Following up the process of making the meaning clearer and more dramatic, some writers go so far as to think and write of some of their ideas as though they were living people with human qualities. This is known as Personification and can often be an effective way of presenting an idea strikingly. Here is the beautiful description of dawn in *Hamlet*:

> See how the morn, in russet mantle clad,
> Walks o'er the dew of yon high eastward hill ...

While here the poet Wordsworth personifies the forces of nature as:

> Wisdom and Spirit of the Universe!
> Thou Soul, that art the eternity of thought ...

And Keats addresses the Grecian Urn, decorated with carvings of ancient Greek religious festivals as:

> Sylvan historian! who canst express
> A flowery tale more sweetly than our rhyme!

SYMBOLISM

A further stage in the use of 'indirect' expression is described as Symbolism. At times in our reading of literature, we come suddenly to recognize that what the writer is presenting and describing is not after all what he is chiefly concerned with; but that there is a hidden or a deeper meaning which, with the help perhaps of slight hints, we are expected to guess. Thus, in his opening chapter of *Bleak House* we come to guess that Dickens' magnificent presentation of London fog is there not only for its own sake but to symbolize the chaos and confusion in the world of human beings, especially around the Law Courts.

> Fog everywhere. Fog up the river where it flows among green aits and meadows; fog down the river, where it rolls defiled among the tiers of shipping, and the waterside pollutions of a great (and dirty) city. Fog on the Essex marshes, fog on the Kentish heights ...
>
> The raw afternoon is rawest, and the dense fog is densest, and the muddy streets are muddiest near that leaden-headed old obstruction, appropriate ornament for the threshold of a leaden-headed old corporation: Temple Bar. And hard by Temple Bar, in Lincolns Inn Hall, at the very heart of the fog, sits the Lord High Chancellor, in his High Court of Chancery.

The sonnet by Keats which begins
'Much have I travelled in the realms of gold
And many goodly states and kingdoms seen ...'

at first seems to be a 'travel' poem, but in line five we come across the name of the writer, Homer, which helps us to realize that the idea of exotic travels in this poem is used to symbolize Keats' mental adventures as he reads famous books. In Hopkins' poem *Windhover* we come to recognize that the soaring kestrel is a symbol of Christ, and in Yeats' *Byzantium* we see that the city of Constantinople becomes a symbol of the perfection and permanence of art.

A warning should be given here about the danger of looking for symbols where they are not intended. Many pieces of writing are clearly limited to the exact presentation of a particular scene or situation, purely for its own sake, and this is an entirely justifiable kind of writing. To persist in seeing symbolism where none is intended can only distort the meaning and purpose of a piece of writing.

IRONY

This is the last of the 'indirect' uses of language which we think it necessary to be ready for. Irony, or the ironical use of language, attempts to convey a certain meaning to us in words which at first sight appear to say exactly the opposite. Unless we read intelligently, and look out for clues; or if we fail to consider the general relation of a passage with what has gone before, we may easily miss the irony. When Swift, in *Gulliver's Travels*, makes Gulliver describe the Parliament of eighteenth-century England in these terms.

> The other part of the Parliament consisted of an assembly called the House of Commons; who were all principal gentlemen, *freely* picked and culled out by the people themselves for their great abilities and love of their country ...

we are soon aware that Swift is implying the very opposite of what he says; and, although he italicized the word 'freely', as a special hint, even without this we should have no difficulty in understanding his implication that M.Ps of that time had no ability, no love of their country, and were by no means the people's own choice!

Thomas Love Peacock in *Crochet Castle* describes a Scottish merchant who has bought a country estate:

> He could not become, like a true born English squire, part and parcel of the barley-giving earth; he could not find in game-bagging, poacher-shooting, trespasser-impounding, footpath-stopping, common-enclosing, rack-renting, and all the other liberal pursuits and pastimes which make a country gentleman an ornament to the world and a blessing to the poor ... modes of filling up his time that accorded with his Caledonian instinct.

We have no difficulty in understanding that 'game-bagging', etc. are *not* regarded by the writer as liberal pursuits but as very *ill*iberal and barbarous ones; and that the English country gentleman was certainly neither an ornament to the world nor a blessing to the poor!

Now we refer to two important aspects of appreciation which are of a different kind from those above.

ALLUSION

Many writers are not able to express their meaning sufficiently by either literal or figurative uses of the language, and seem instinctively to discuss it or develop it by alluding or referring to all sorts of related topics, covering a wide range of knowledge sometimes very unrelated to the main subject. We can only hope that the student can keep up, or at least that he knows how to use various reference books, dictionaries of quotations, and so on. Something of the meaning is of course usually to be inferred from the context. Consider;

> So excellent a king that was to this
> Hyperion to a satyr ...
>
> *Hamlet*

or

> The distinction between 'journalism' and 'literature' is quite futile, unless we are drawing such violent contrasts as that between Gibbon's *History* and tonight's evening paper.
>
> T. S. Eliot, 1931

or

> At the beginning there was a huge drop of milk.
> Then Doondari came and he created the stone.
> Then the stone created iron;
> And iron created fire ...
>
> *A Fulani creation myth*

If we are studying a specially prescribed book, of course, we hope that the editor will have provided the necessary background information; if we are tackling any examination test involving an 'unseen' passage we must hope that the examiners have had a fair sense of what students at the given stage may be expected to know.

FORM

Finally it is often important to consider the effect on a piece of writing of its general form. Its 'form' is quite literally its shape as a whole; in other words, the pattern of construction and arrangement, which determine the word order, sentence formation, rhythmic structure into which the whole passage has been fitted. In the field of poetry this question may seem easier to deal with, because again we have a number of ready-made terms, such as Stanzas, Ballad, Couplet, Sonnet, Blank Verse, etc. which seems to save us a good deal of trouble. However, even in the field of poetry we should not be content to take things too easily, and in fact it does not help our appreciation very deeply merely to observe that a particular piece of writing has been cast into the form of a sonnet. We must be able to explain the effect which the form contributes to the piece as a whole; how conveniently, for example, does it mark the stages of the development of a passage? How boldly does it bring out the plan and the impact of the whole? How conveniently does it underline the emotional effect intended? ... and so on.

The Sonnet, for example, is a fourteen-lined poem; often divided into two sections of eight and six lines in which the first eight may present a situation, while the final six express the poet's thoughts. Sometimes it falls into three groups of four lines, each presenting a different phase of an argument, to be summed up in a final couplet at the end. But what is the essential *form* of the following rather unusual sonnet by Shakespeare? Observe how it is used to give the impression of the poet's long drawn out frustrations and despairs, which nevertheless he must endure in order not to leave his love 'alone'.

> Tired with all these, for restful Death I cry,
> As to behold desert a beggar born,
> And needing nothing trimmed in jollity,
> And purest faith unhappily forsworn,
> And gilded honour shamefully misplaced,
> And maiden virtue rudely strumpeted,
> And right perfection wrongfully disgraced,
> And strength by limping sway disabled
> And art made tongue-tied by authority,
> And folly – doctor-like – controlling skill,
> And simple truth miscalled simplicity,
> And captive good attending captain ill:
> > Tired with all these, from these would I be gone,
> > Save that, to die, I leave my love alone.

Prose is less often cast into a recognizable or set form; nevertheless aspects of form can often be seen in the repetition of particular word or sentence patterns; the recurrence of symbols. We should also note whether the sentences are highly-controlled in structure, whether they are short and broken, whether they flow on as though representing the flow of thought, of conversation, of internal monologue. But in the case of prose, again, we shall always seek not merely to describe what we observe in the way of formal pattern, but to explain its effect.

Compare for example the different prose 'form' represented by the two following passages.

> Reading maketh a full man; conference a ready man; and writing an exact man. And therefore, if a man write little he had need have a great memory; if he confer little, he had need have a present wit; and if he read little he had need have much cunning, to seem to know that he doth not. Histories make men wise; poets, witty; the mathematics subtle; natural philosophy, deep; moral, grave; logic and rhetoric, able to contend.

Here Bacon, in his Essay *Of Studies*, is concerned to analyze his thoughts as exactly and economically as possible, without any ornament or decoration; so his sentences are as brief and condensed as possible, yet still arranged in a pattern (reading conference, writing: writing, conference, reading) to show his methodical approach. The last sentence of twenty words, it will be noticed, is really six short sentences, gaining great brevity from sharing in the same structure. Now compare this passage from Joyce's *Portrait of the Artist as a Young Man* in which an Irish priest is trying to convey the idea of 'eternity' to some schoolboys:

> You have often seen the sand on the sea shore. How fine are its tiny grains! And how many of these tiny grains go to make up the small handful which a child grasps in its play. Now imagine a mountain of that sand, a million miles high, reaching from the earth to the farthest heavens, and a million miles broad, extending to remotest, and a million miles in thickness, and imagine such an enormous mass of countless particles of sand multiplied as often as there are

leaves in the forest, drops of water in the mighty ocean, feathers on birds, scales on fish, hairs on animals, atoms in the vast expanse of the air, and imagine that at the end of every million years a little bird came to that mountain and carried away in its beak a tiny grain of that sand. How many millions upon millions of centuries would pass before that bird had carried away even a square foot of that mountain, how many eons upon eons before it had carried it all away? Yet at the end of that immense stretch of time not even one instant of eternity could be said to have ended.

You will appreciate here how the passage begins with several short homely sentences to introduce the subject, but then the sentences swell out, with phrase piled upon phrase, clause upon clause, as if to reflect the immensity of the subject being presented.

Judgement

Now, having surveyed in detail both the subject-matter and its treatment, we come to the final stage, of Judgement. The good student will feel a natural desire, after spending some time on a piece of writing, to express some kind of final opinion about it. In a public examination the question may, or may not, seem to ask for something of this kind, but it is a very good thing at the end of an exercise in appreciation to indicate as clearly as one can a considered opinion about the passage studied.

It is helpful to think of this, perhaps, as rather like a vote of thanks given to a visitor who has come to give an address to a special society or institution. As most students will know, a good vote of thanks may well be quite brief. It should certainly be sincere: conventional eulogies carry little conviction, and reflect no credit either on the person who makes them or on the person to whom they are addressed. Also, of course, the vote of thanks should refer appropriately to matters of special interest or distinctive features contained in the address.

Thus, in the literary field, a final judgement cannot take any set form, because it will be adjusted to the particular passage which has just been under examination. It will be a direct reflection of the insight, maturity, reading, experience, and capacity for generalization of the individual student. It should, of course, be more than a summary of all that has already been said, though it should be in accordance with the detailed observations that have been made.

Two useful hints in this connection are, firstly that judgements can sometimes be made effectively with the help of comparisons. An example might be: 'This poem is certainly as relevant to the young African today as Arnold's *Dover Beach* was to the harassed intellectual of the mid-nineteenth century, or Eliot's *Ash Wednesday* was to the even more harassed intellectual of the 1930s!'. Secondly it should be remembered that judgements may involve some balancing of conflicting views: 'the truth', in Oscar Wilde's famous epigram, 'is rarely pure and never simple'. So a final judgement may well take some such form as:

> This passage is obviously written on an urgent problem, but we do not ...

or

> Although this is a much overused theme in modern poetry, nevertheless we must admit ...

or

> The writer of this poem is obviously an enthusiastic artist in words, but he has neglected ...

Now we have discussed and illustrated the chief elements of technique which may help us to recognize the effect of any piece of writing and to form some kind of a judgement about it. Let us set out these elements:

> LOGICAL STRUCTURE
> CHOICE OF WORDS
> SOUND OF WORDS
> WORD ORDER
> RHYTHM
> SIMILE AND METAPHOR
> SYMBOLISM
> IRONY
> ALLUSION
> FORM

The question now arises as to how this scheme can best be used.

Certainly the scheme needs to be used with insight and discretion; the appreciation of such a delicate thing as a piece of literature is not merely a matter of going through and sifting out a number of constituent elements, in the way that an oil chemist may analyze the contents of a specimen of crude oil. In the early stages of learning 'appreciation', it may well be worth while to examine a passage for anything worth saying under any of the above ten headings, just to make sure that no important aspects have been overlooked. But we must always remember that literary appreciation is essentially an integrating, a constructive process. It involves analysis but it also involves synthesis, a 'building-together'. Even further, it involves the art of seeing things in the full accuracy of their detail, and yet at the same time *seeing the details as part of a far more important whole*. The kind of statement, alas! sometimes seen in examination answers, which is of little value indeed goes something like this, '... the poem also contains some good expressions, excellent choice of words, and much symbolism'. Such a statement is of little value because it lacks precision. It glosses over essential details rather than points them out.

So far we have been setting out the tools of analysis, but we hope and expect that students using the book will learn far more of the essence of this skill of literary appreciation by seeing the tools in use – just as students of surgery in Medical Schools spend a great deal of time, not only in reading textbooks and looking at diagrams, but in watching their surgeon-teachers at work on real operations. In the following pages we take a number of pieces of writing of various kinds and conduct our own examination and appreciation of them.

The appreciation of these passages is possibly longer and more detailed than most students will have time for in actual examination conditions, but it seems best to do the job as thoroughly as possible so that students may acquire as much insight as possible.

Demonstrations

To make best use of this
section we suggest that
students should read, think
about and if possible, discuss
each passage before looking
at the Demonstration provided

1 Love Song
(from the Amharic)

You lime of the forest, honey among the rocks,
Lemon of the cloister, grape in the savannah.
A hip to be enclosed by one hand;
A thigh round like a piston.
Your back – a manuscript to read hymns from.
Your eye trigger-happy shoots heroes.
Your gown cobweb tender,
Your skirt like soothing balm.
Soap? Oh no, you wash in Arabian scent,
Your calf painted in silver lines.
I dare not touch you!
Hardly dare to look back,
You mistress of my body,
More precious to me than my hand or my foot.
Like the fruit of the valley, the water of paradise.
Flower of the night: wrought by divine craftsmen;
With muscular thigh she stepped on my heart,
Her eternal heel trod me down.
But have no compassion with me:
Her breast resembles the finest gold;
When she opens her heart –
The Saviour image!
And Jerusalem herself, sacred city,
Shouts 'holy holy'!

Demonstration

This poem, though a translation from the traditional language of the ancient Christian kingdom of Ethiopia, gives us a fairly straightforward and enjoyable beginning to our studies in appreciation. When we see the title, we should avoid jumping to the conclusion that we know exactly what the poem has to tell us: the field of 'love poems', up and down and across the world, has embraced a wide variety of moods and experiences, all within the general relationship of 'love'. Also love poems have prompted writers to experiment with many different methods of approach and presentation. To what extent is this a Song? we may ask: but we shall postpone the question until later in our examination of the poem.

The situation, the development, and intention of this poem are quite easy to grasp. The writer is a lover who thinks of his beloved, picturing her in his mind, and trying to find adequate words to express what he feels about her. We note that the poem is not merely *descriptive* in spite of many of the vivid phrases it contains: it is to a great extent subjective, being mainly concerned with the writer's feelings. To what extent could an artist actually draw an *exact* picture of the beloved from the information given in the poem?

The development of the poem is a series of attempts to find suitable comparisons to express his admiration and awe of the lady. His attempts move towards climax, each in turn becoming more desperate and exaggerated than the previous one. The poem ends on the most daring note of all, when the writer borrows ideas and expressions from religion to convey his abject dependence upon her for his survival. We may perhaps know the disillusioned comment by one of the characters in Shakespeare's play *As you Like It*:

> Men have died from time to time, and worms have eaten them, but not for love.

Nevertheless, most people (we hope) have some experience of the anxiety and torment of the young lover – Shakespeare himself, of course, embodied his knowledge of such feelings in *Romeo and Juliet*. In our present poem, we must admire the resourcefulness of the writer in his search for ideas to give us the equivalent of his own desperate passion. The comparisons he makes are not at all 'literary': they are not borrowed from the language of conventional European, American or Arabic love poetry (though they suggest something of the lively improvization of the West Indian *Calypso*. All his comparisons come from the realities of the writer's own African background, which now, of course, includes the engineering technology that is part of the environment of human beings all the world over.

Befitting the impetuosity of youth, the poem has no preamble or introduction, but plunges immediately into its subject:

> You lime of the forest, honey among the rocks
> Lemon of the cloister, grape in the savannah.

These lines give us a sharp contrast, four times repeated, between the sweetness (though often combined with a certain sharpness) of fruit (or honey), which is always most gratefully appreciated in circumstances of harshness, barrenness, drought.

The mind of the writer then leaves the search for comparisons for a moment to contemplate the body of the beloved, and we understand something of her slimness and her physical perfection through the simile comparing her thigh to the piston of an engine, in which the exactness of shape is essential to the efficiency of the machine. A rapid change in the direction of his thoughts next compares her back to a manuscript to read hymns from, and calls up the picture of a devoted worshipper painstakingly making out the words of a hymn written in manuscript. It seems that the writer hardly dares to look upon the face of the beloved; and indeed, when he moves round from the back to confront the lady's eye, how devastating is the effect! Here we have an allusion to the 'Western' type of 'cowboy' story or film, in which the hero is usually a fabulous gunman, a 'dead-shot', who can subdue any number of opponents in a split second. Thus the writer conveys to us how his courage fails as he thinks of meeting the lady face to face.

Now his thoughts dwell upon her gown, which also partakes of her magical, unearthly quality, being 'cobweb-soft'. From its association with her, it seems more soft and delicate than any cloth ever made, or worn, before by human beings. From her garments, his eye next falls upon her exposed arm or shoulder, perhaps. Is this normal human flesh? he wonders – washed by such a homely article as soap? No, impossible! When this divine and exquisite creature purifies her lovely body it can only be with the rarest of fine perfumes – such as that from Arabia. (Can we guess that there is here an allusion to Lady Macbeth's cry, expressing the indelible nature of the crime she has committed: All the perfumes of Arabia will not sweeten this little hand? Maybe our anonymous writer clearly shows the omnivorous instinct for comparison and allusion which students of literature will specially associate with the English poets of the seventeenth century.) Nevertheless the poet keeps us closely in touch with African realities by the mention of the beautifying silver lines painted on the lady's calf, though whether we should think of these as actual or metaphorical is not quite certain.

Now come a number of plain, bare statements, the more effective as they follow the previous highly-coloured ideas, starkly expressing the writer's awe and submission – his complete self-dedication, to the lady. She is the 'mistress' of his body, more precious to him than his hand or his foot. The next series of comparisons has a rather different feature: the lady is compared less to real, actual things, and more to religious and mythical ideas. She is likened to 'the water of paradise' – a particularly potent, meaningful concept in the middle of a dry, rocky landscape; to the kind of flower which blooms, almost miraculously, in the night without help from the sun, its penetrating colour and fragrance standing out impressively in the darkness; something beyond the capacity of mere mortal human beings to produce, 'wrought by divine craftsmen'. Note the plural here, suggesting that the perfection of the lady is the result not of a single creator, but of the labours of a whole team of craftsmen. (We may detect a strong correspondence to some of the lines of William Blake's famous poem – not at all a love poem – *Tyger*:

> What immortal hand or eye
> Could produce thy fearful symmetry?

Just as Blake felt the tiger to be bound up with the mysterious powers which keep the universe in motion, so the Amharic poet sees his beloved as one of the divine mysteries of creation.) All the more easy to understand why her 'eternal heel', her superhuman powers, cast him into despair and dejection. How, he feels, can such a divine, elevated, creature have 'compassion' on a mere mortal like him? Significantly, we notice that as his awe of the lady increases, the poet drops the use of the 'second person' (you) which suggests a certain degree of intimacy, and continues in the 'third person' (she), which indicates greater detachment. It is interesting to note that in some African cultures the use of the third person is customary, sometimes even compulsory, when addressing a person of superior rank.

To bring the poem to a memorable close, the writer saves the most potent comparison of all. The lines become shorter, signifying a kind of breathlessness. The comparison is no longer introduced formally as a simile or metaphor. The beloved is thought of, in a tremendous hyperbole, as a kind of sacred shrine, a Holy of Holies, a Kabba, and the lover himself becomes a pilgrim who has disciplined himself and travelled far in hope of a vision of his deity. While the outside of the shrine may be as beautiful and fine as gold, when the shrine itself is opened at the great festival, or for a privileged worshipper, the blessedness is out of this world: the beholder cannot attempt to describe in detail the beauty or the splendour of what he sees: it is a 'mystery' beyond the powers of human expression – the image of his Saviour, the power which redeems his life from disorder, disaster and meaninglessness. A rich tissue of religious allusions is evoked by the words of the poem, chiefly Christian, but not without meaning to other religions, as we think of the great occasions when priests and prophets have been granted momentary visions of the full nature of their God:

> And I John saw the heavenly city the new
> Jerusalem coming down from God out of heaven,
> prepared as a bride for her husband
>
> *Revelation* Ch. 2.

In the two final lines, the picture broadens out, and we see not only the individual worshipper but the heavenly host, the princes of the morning, the dwellers in the city of Jerusalem – indeed perhaps the whole world, congregated about the shrine, in ecstatic reverence, making the heavens re-echo with their hymns of praise. Beyond this the poem does not take us; as though the lover, the worshipper, perhaps lapses into unconsciousness after the intensity of his devotion.

We have already noted that the poem is described to us as a Song, in its original language. Certainly in its English translation it seems to have lost that quality, for as the poem stands it is notable for the terseness and directness of its language, which is much nearer to drama than to singing. Certainly its interest to us is much more in the urgency and novelty of the thoughts than in any abstract pattern of musical word arrangement.

Our conclusion is that this is a poem of rich meaning and powerful passion, communicated very effectively, but without the use of many of the more traditional poetic devices.

2 Song: 'Ask Me No More...

Ask me no more, where Jove bestows,
When June is past, the fading rose:
For in your Beauties orient deep
These flowers, as in their causes, sleep.

Ask me no more, whither do stray
The golden atoms of the day:
For in pure love heaven did prepare
Those powders to enrich your hair.

Ask me no more, whither doth haste
The Nightingale, when May is past:
For in your sweet dividing throat
She winters, and keeps warm her note.

Ask me no more, where those stars light,
That downwards fall in dead of night:
For in your eyes they sit, and there
Fixed, become as in their sphere.

Ask me no more, if east or west
The Phoenix builds her spicy nest:
For unto you at last she flies,
And in your fragrant bosom dies.

NOTES line 1 *Jove* King of Gods (Roman) i.e. Lord and Creator of the universe.
2 *Causes* (philosophical): first causes, or origins.
6 *Atoms* The small particles sometimes seen in a ray of sunlight.
11 *Dividing* A musical term of the seventeenth century: harmonious.
16 *Sphere* (philosophical): natural element.
18 *Phoenix* Legendary Arabian bird – symbol of life. Only one existed, and a new one was born from the ashes of the previous one.

Demonstration

This seventeenth-century English poem (another 'Song' it will be noticed) is here provided with several notes to assist students to grasp some of the ideas which may be outside the general run of modern knowledge, whether to a native-English *or* a second-language speaker. In addition to these references, we shall observe a few language usages which are no longer in customary use (e.g. whither ... do stray ... doth haste ... unto), but essentially the ideas and language of the poem are not difficult.

What can we discover of the 'situation'? The writer, or the speaker, in the poem is requesting us repeatedly to 'Ask him no more' certain questions; such as what happens to the rose when June is past; where do the golden atoms of the day wander to; where does the nightingale go after the month of May; where do falling (i.e. shooting) stars end up; where does the birth of the new Phoenix take place? Why, we may ask, should the poet no longer wish to find answers to these questions? But first, what kind of questions are they, and with what degree of seriousness should we ponder about them? We may feel that they are the kind of naïve questions which children ask their parents (Where did I come from? Why is water wet? Why is the sky up?); or better still, we may recognize them as the kind of speculative, metaphysical questions which used to be asked and discussed at great length by the philosophers and poets of pre-scientific times: the sprinkling of medieval philosophic terms in the poem confirms this. Why, then, does the poet no longer wish to be asked such questions? Because he now knows the answers to them, and they are matters of certainty, no longer open to discussion! In fact, he answers the questions for us, each in turn; we notice the introduction of the second person pronoun, and the references to beauty and various human attributes, and we should be very dull not to guess that this is another 'love poem', and that it is being addressed to the lady who commands the poet's admiration. The poem gives us no indication of an outward, physical *situation* of any kind; there is no mention of time, place, actual meeting, social occasion, or anything like that. It seems to be completely *internal* concerned with the expression of the writer's feelings and thought;

and we soon recognize that this is the kind of poem which the poet writes to his beloved, to express his affection, to convey his unsatisfied longings, to flatter her, and ultimately to win her favours. It could be called a 'praise poem', though the praise in this case is given in a somewhat indirect way, and needs a little careful unravelling. The poem has a very noticeable regular form, which we shall study later, and the *development* consists mainly of the series of questions the poet no longer wishes to be asked, followed by the answers to them he has now discovered. We sense a slow growth or development as we read from stanza to stanza, and the poem ends on a note of climax, with the feeling that there is no more to be said on the subject.

Now that we have traced the general outline of the poem, we can begin to fill in the details, and to interpret the sense more exactly. What happens to the fading, or dying rose after its season of flourishing? is the first question. In more general terms, what becomes of the beauty of a living thing such as a flower, which attains its perfection for only a brief time? The beauty of a flower is obviously very real, very unmistakable, while it lasts. Can it be that it merely vanishes, or evaporates, as though it had never existed? No, says the poet: we need not debate this question: I know the answer. All these flowers, and all their beauty, after fading and withering return to You, and become part of Your beauty; indeed, Your beauty is the 'cause' or origin from which they sprung in the first place.

'What nonsense!' the hard-hearted, practical-minded reader may exclaim. How could this possibly happen? It is contrary to common sense, and to all our modern knowledge of natural phenomena. Of course. Yet this first stanza leads us to consider a special use of language which is quite often found in poetry. In such cases the writer is not really trying to describe for us the exact phenomena of the world of reality: his mind is 'playing with' ideas and speculations, in a fanciful, even fantastic way, with the object not of conveying to us the factual truth of a situation, but the truth (or urgency) of a feeling. Perhaps in this case the title 'Song: …' warns us not to take the factual basis of the poem too seriously, or too literally.

So, by this imaginative conception (or 'conceit' – as it was sometimes called in the seventeenth century) of the beauty of the 'rose' being added to the beauty of the beloved, he gives an indirect but powerful impression of the tremendous fascination her beauty has for him; '*the* rose', according to the exact words of the poem is a general expression and refers to all flowers: the conceit indicates appreciation of the lady's physical perfection, but it also seems to have a more profound significance quite beyond the merely sensual appeal.

If we have now found how to accept this imaginative conception, we can now go on to the next stanza, in which we 'learn' that all those tiny scintillating particles sometimes seen in a ray of sunlight do not float about the world without a purpose. Heaven (we notice here how the writer jumps from 'Jove' to 'Heaven', from Rome to Christianity without any hesitation) – 'heaven', he imagines, has prepared these tiny fragments, those 'powders' to increase the glory of the lady's hair. Then again, the nightingale, after the month of May when it can be heard singing abroad in woods and forests, returns to the lady, as it were, hibernates in her throat, preserving and cherishing ('keeping warm') her musical voice (her note). The lady's voice is not of course, an exact replica of the nightingale's beautiful song, but, in a subdued form, it seems to contain many of the same beautiful qualities.

The exact nature of 'falling stars' was endlessly discussed by philosophers of ancient times: now every schoolboy probably knows that they are fragments of solid matter flying through space until they burn themselves up on entering the earth's atmosphere. According to the poet's imagination, however, these 'falling stars' do not 'light' i.e. alight, or just disappear into nothingness: in some supernatural way, they end their careers in the eyes of the beloved, where they seem to find their best and their entirely proper setting. This we now have no difficulty in interpreting, not as a statement valid in the field of natural science, but as a flattering comment on the deep mysterious beauty which flashes, or sparkles, out of the lady's eyes.

Finally, the Phoenix, most famous of legendary birds; a symbol of the mysterious renewal of life which has fascinated men throughout the ages, and which has appeared in many different forms, for example, in the mystery of Christ, whose death by crucifixion signifies to Christians the bringing of new life to the world. (Incidentally, the Phoenix was adopted as a personal emblem by the famous prophet-novelist D. H. Lawrence.) We no longer need to speculate, the poet tells us, exactly where the miraculous rebirth of the Phoenix takes place (whether 'east or west'). This miracle of nature is in You: it *is* You. You are the source from which the whole of life in the future will spring. This again is the poet's indirect way of expressing his reverence for the beloved, his complete dependence upon her. Who would not be gratified, or flattered, by such a sequence of compliments!

Now, having carried out this amount of brain-work upon the poem, the student should read it over again and ask himself really sincerely how he responds to it. Is it 'far-fetched', out-of-date, nonsensical, absolutely unacceptable? Surprisingly few readers will feel like this; most, on the contrary, will find it a fascinating poem which runs through the mind long after the study of it has ceased. To explain how this happens, we have to look at some other aspects of the poet's technique.

Apart from the basic imaginative conception of the poem, there are no incidental similes, metaphors, or other figures of speech. The choice of words is on the whole unspectacular: considering that the poem is dealing with female beauty, the absence of adjectives is remarkable. A number of subtle, but powerful points, however, come to our attention. Consider, for example, the fine phrase 'Your Beauties orient deep'. In spite of a slight grammatical ambiguity here: – is 'orient' a noun following 'Beauty's' in the possessive case; or is it a kind of adverb qualifying 'deep'? – we relish the association of the lady's Beauty with the rich train of ideas which cluster around the word 'orient', suggesting the East, exotic far-away lands of romance and splendour, the sunrise, the orient pearl, etc. Then although it refers primarily to the small particles of dust seen in a ray of sunlight, the phrase

        the golden atoms of the day

also suggests, perhaps even more to the modern reader than to the original readers, some of the intensely pure elemental substances from which the universe ('the day') is built up. The 'warmth' of the nightingale hibernating in the lady's throat and the 'fragrance' of her bosom, suggestive of the 'spicy nest' of the Phoenix, also add significant immediacy to our sense of the lady's physical reality.

But the chief cause of the success of this poem comes from a different aspect of technique. Although our *mind* has to be active in interpretating the ideas of the poem, and might be inclined to rebel, it is at the same time charmed, put under a spell, by the easy, graceful rhythm and the exquisitely shaped stanza pattern. This poem has obviously been written by a skilful versifier; one who has the ability to select and combine words in a way which seems absolutely natural, and yet delightfully 'artificial'. While we do not neglect the meaning of the poem, we are at the same time pleasantly aware of the regular pattern of rhythm, and the correspondence of sound which is one of the ancient, traditional pleasures of poetry. Each stanza closely matches the general pattern: each contains two pairs of end-rhyming words which are full and sonorous: we notice that almost all the rhyming words are based not on sharp short vowel sounds, but, sustained and resounding, on the extended English dipthongs:

ou	– bestow : rose	throat : note
εə	– prepare : hair	there : sphere
ei	– stray : day	
ai	– light : night	flies : dies

Each line of the poem contains eight syllables with four stresses, and the basic pattern is iambic (–/–/–/–/) without ever becoming mechanical or over-obvious. Each line divides into two halves at almost exactly the same place; but against this slight pause, the sense at the end of each line runs on quite quickly. The metrical pattern we may say *underlies* and serves the natural colloquial stresses of the poet's voice as we seem to hear him speaking the poem to us. The poem is aptly described as a Song, in the sense that the mere commonplace words from which it is constructed seem to take on a higher, more musical quality than they normally have – though whether this is a poem which could be improved by actually being sung aloud is doubtful: so much is already gained by the confident nuances of the poet's speaking voice. As we read the poem over and over again, it is apparent at every point how each word seems to drop inevitably into place, making its own contribution in itself, and yet contributing perfectly to the whole:

> Ask me no more, / where Jove bestows,
> When June is past / the fading rose: /
> For in your Beauties / orient deep /
> These flowers, / as in their causes, / sleep ...

Yet, we should be quite clear that the perfection of the poem does not consist alone in the smooth, even, musical *arrangement* of the words. It depends on the fact that the beauty and elegance of technique in the poem so perfectly fit the beauty and elegance of its purpose, its supreme tribute to the beauty of womanhood.

3 Zulu Girl

When in the sun the hot red acres smoulder,
Down where the sweating gang its labour plies,
A girl flings down her hoe, and from her shoulder
Unslings her child tormented by the flies.

She takes him to a ring of shadow pooled
By thorn trees: purpled with the blood of ticks
While her sharp nails, in slow caresses ruled,
Prowl through his hair with sharp electric clicks.

His sleepy mouth, plugged by the heavy nipple,
Tugs like a puppy, grunting as he feeds:
Through his frail nerves her own deep languors ripple
Like a broad river sighing through its reeds.

Yet in that drowsy stream her flesh imbibes
An old unquenched unsmotherable heat –
The curbed ferocity of beaten tribes,
The sullen dignity of their defeat.

Her body looms above him like a hill
Within whose shade a village lies at rest,
Or the first cloud so terrible and still
That bears the coming harvest in its breast.

Demonstration

The title of this poem immediately gives us a direct clue to the 'situation'. 'Zulu' directs our thoughts to South Africa, and in the opening three lines we are shown 'the sun', the 'hot red acres', 'the sweating gang', and this conveys to us at once a scene on an African farm. It is not, of course, a native African farm; in fact the adverb 'Down' in line 2 suggests that the scene is viewed from 'up above' somewhere, possibly from the farmhouse of a settler, or by a rider on horseback looking down from a hill. The word 'gang', as of course frequently used in this connection, suggests that its members have no individuality, are treated rather like prisoners, or are being made to undertake forced labour: certainly they have no personal pride or pleasure in the work they are doing, and are actually under some kind of compulsion.

As we begin to observe the scene, our attention is caught by one particular girl who has flung down her hoe, and we see that she is carrying a baby on her back which she proceeds to 'unsling'. The child, beside being 'tormented by flies', is also in need of nourishment, for the girl takes him to a patch of thin shade near by to feed him at her breast. While the child feeds, the girl passes her hand caressingly through his hair – it is significant perhaps that the mother is referred to as a 'girl'; this may suggest that she is not a 'wife' and belongs to the vast number of black South Africans who have lost their traditional ways of life and been caught up in the chaos of the modern world. It is also possible to suggest that there is an element of hardship and the lack of a supporting social system in the fact that the girl is forced to carry the child on her back while she herself is working in the hot sun – though this may be customary in some African cultures.

Here we have the basic situation in the poem. No other characters or events enter directly into it: it is merely a mother going to feed her baby. The scene is a normal and fundamental one. But let us now examine its development. As we read on through stanzas three, four, and five we see that the poet goes on to give his impression of the relationship and feeling between mother and child, in more than a merely physical sense. The child is 'grunting' as he feeds, that is he is feeding greedily and expressing his simple but deep satisfaction. Not only does he take in physical nourishment, however, for during this process of feeding, her own deep feelings 'ripple' and are conveyed little by little into his frail, infantile nerves. The poem admirably suggests the strong intimate mother-and-child relationship developed by breast-feeding (often, of course, lost or destroyed in more 'advanced' cultures). The word 'languors' is important; it should be easily interpreted, especially with reference to its more common adjectival form 'languid'. It tells us that the girl appears rather weary, unenthusiastic, hopeless, as though expressing a deep despair and resentment against the whole situation in which she finds herself. Nevertheless, even in her mood of hopelessness, her motherhood and the latent satisfaction she has in feeding her child, seem to arouse in her a kind of pride, 'the old unquenched, unsmotherable heat': a feeling perhaps that her life has some value, that she is taking part in an important life process; that she is not alone and abandoned; she belongs to an old enduring tradition of human struggle and survival; her 'tribes' though 'curbed' and 'beaten' for the time being, 'have a dignity' in their 'defeat'; and still retain their self-respect, and are ready to 'rise again'. As the poem develops, we seem to move gradually closer to the mother, until in the final stanza we are looking up at her, almost as though through the eyes of the child himself: and she appears as an impressive, statuesque figure, shielding and protecting her helpless infant. In the two last lines of all, after being compared to a 'hill', she is likened to a great storm cloud which

bears the coming harvest in its breast.

Although, in the prose sense, this is not explained very fully or exactly, the storm cloud, at present 'terrible and still', but full of menace, invites us to look ahead in the future to the possibility of harvest, which can come only after the storms of the wet season; – could the harvest possibly be the revival of the oppressed African tribes?

Now we have, in fact, arrived at the intention of the poem. Without appealing to our emotions very directly or blatantly (as a propagandist might have done) the writer arouses our sympathy for the Zulu Girl in the hardships of her existence; this leads on to an admiration for her endurance and for the strength of life that is seen in her. This in its turn, through the concluding simile, leads to a kind of prophetic hint that the scene we have witnessed is not final, and that a different and better state of affairs is bound to come in the future. We notice that this hope is not conveyed by plain, prose statement, as a matter of fact: it is glimpsed imaginatively by the poet's intuition and conveyed in the form of this indirect suggestion.

Like many other poems, this one begins with a fairly simple observed situation, and as the poet develops and reflects upon it, its references broaden out until it is of world-wide significance.

In interpreting the poem thus far, we have already noticed some aspects of its technique. But let us now look back and examine, or *appreciate*, in more detail how the effects have been so skilfully managed. The first strong impression we are given in the poem is of the heat which scorches the landscape where the girl is working: the acres, we are told, are red, which we know is the predominant colour of the African earth, but 'hot red', an obvious pair of adjectives, suggests in our mind something similar – 'red hot', the epithet usually applied to heated iron. This together with the metaphor of 'smoulder' gives the impression that the land is almost too hot to bear, and could almost burst into flames. We are given other details which emphasize the unpleasant nature of the 'gang's' work: they are 'sweating'; the child is 'tormented by the flies'. At last she 'flings down' her hoe. Note she does not just 'drop it' or throw it down: the word 'flings' suggests impatience and exasperation. An interesting point to notice in the first stanza is the way in which the rhythmic and rhyming pattern emphasizes the physical effort made by the girl when she takes the child from her back.

When in the sun the hot red acres *smoulder*
....
A girl flings down her hoe, and from her *shoulder*
Unslings her child, (tormented by the flies)

'Shoulder' is in an emphatic position because it rhymes with 'smoulder'; this encourages us to make a slight pause in thought and in reading before we continue with the next line, so that the verb

59

Unslings (rhyming internally with *flings*) comes with the effect of a violent jerk. Since the word 'flies' at the end of the stanza is also placed as a rhyming word (following 'plies') this brings sharper attention to the unpleasantness of the torment the child has been suffering from the insects.

In stanza two, we read how the mother, in the meagre shade of the thorn trees, is searching the hair of her child for ticks – again a detail which suggest the poverty and insanitary conditions under which these labourers live. We notice that her sharp nails are 'purpled with the blood' of the parasites. In fact, the phrase 'purpled with the blood of ticks' is grammatically out of place; it is intended presumably to relate to its head-word 'nails', but the nails are introduced by the conjunction 'while' and cannot strictly be governed by a loose phrase which lies outside the clause altogether. Nevertheless, this slight dislocation of syntax is easily forgiven as our attention is held by the metaphor 'prowled', which suggests that her fingers are like a fierce animal searching through the forest for its prey. The sharp electric clicks are produced when she finds a tick and cracks it between her finger nails: this produces a sound like that given by an electric spark (as from a car battery). Not only does the metaphor give this impression but the sounds of the word sequence '*ticks*, elec*tric*, c*licks*' intensify it.

In stanza three, we turn to different matters, but the choice of words is apt again. We see, and hear that the baby's mouth is '*plugged*'; he *tug*s at the nipple: g*run*ting as he feeds. The sequence of *ug*ly vowel sounds suggest the greediness (and hunger) of the baby as he feeds, and this is intensified in the animal simile 'like a *puppy*', in which the same vowel sound appears. Then the poet goes on to describe the deep strong feelings which pass in a steady, inevitable flow from the mother to the child, and here the simile of the broad river is very suitable, its effect being further strengthened by the predominance of broad syllables and diphthongs in the line:

Like a *broad* river *sigh*ing *through* its *reed*s

which well suggests the flow of a mighty river.

Stanza four arouses our increased attention with an unexpected switch of thought, almost a paradox. In the physical sense it is obviously the child which is drinking from its mother: in another sense we are now told that *her* flesh is, in a deeper sense, imbibing something from that drowsy stream. To mark the sudden change of thought from the reflective to the aggressive, there is a sudden change in the rhythmic and sound qualities of this stanza, and we come to a vigorous climax on the energetic multi-syllabic word 'unsmotherable':

> Yet in that drowsy stream her flesh imbibes
> An old unquenched *unsmotherable* heat –

The word 'unsmotherable' takes on special force in its context with 'unquenched', which seem to prepare the way, and the monosyllable 'heat' which gives the line its decisive conclusion. The line as a whole is an emphatic statement of the unquenchable vigour and spirit of the African people: nothing can blot out or obliterate their primal energy (heat – one of the basic essentials of life). The feeling of conviction is repeated in a slightly different rhythmic pattern in two following and closely parallel lines:

> The cur*b*ed ferocity of *b*eaten tribes
> The sullen *d*ignity of their *d*efeat

when an element of alliteration ('b' and 'd') also adds to the forceful pattern of speech.

The poem now moves to its prophetic climax and the Zulu Girl, as we have seen, takes on the significance of a symbol. She is no longer just a single, stray, exploited, hardworking individual in some remote part of the veld: she represents to us the potentiality of her race for suffering, survival, and triumph. Her body is grand and imposing: it 'looms' over her child, and its protective power is beautifully shown in the picturesque simile of

> ... a hill
> Within whose shade a village lies at rest

We notice that the shade, unlike that of the thorn trees (a mere 'pool') is unbroken and extensive, and in it the village lies in peace and tranquillity, 'at rest'. The 'looming hill' leads our thoughts to the second simile of the great thunder cloud, 'so terrible and still', which suggest violent storms to come in the near future, but with the prospect of a welcome harvest in the fullness of time.

'Zulu Girl' is thus an effective and meaningful short poem, in which many resources of the poet's art have been combined to treat one of the urgent problems of the modern world.

4 Ozymandias

I met a traveller from an antique land
Who said: 'Two vast and trunkless legs of stone
Stand in the desert ... . Near them on the sand
Half-sunk, a shattered visage lies, whose frown
And wrinkled lip, and sneer of cold command
Tell that its sculptor well those passions read
Which yet survive, stamped on those lifeless things
The hand that mocked them, and the heart that fed.
And on the pedestal these words appear:
My name is Ozymandias, King of Kings
Look on my works, ye Mighty, and despair.
Nothing beside remains. Round the decay
Of that colossal wreck, boundless and bare,
The lone and level sands stretch far away.'

Demonstration

It does not take long to put together some of the obvious narrated details of this poem '... traveller ... legs of stone ... desert ... shattered visage ... sneer ... pedestal ... 'My name is Ozymandias' ... lone and level sands.' Even without puzzling too much about *exactly* the way the words are fitted together, we begin to form a picture of a desert landscape, and in it the remains of a great statue, which once must have depicted in large proportions a great king or ruler. Now only the legs are left standing, and most of the other parts of the body have disappeared, or are unrecognizable. One detail that the traveller particularly observed, however, were the fragments of the face. Although 'shattered' the face retained a very lifelike expression, and it was possible to recognize the 'frown', the 'wrinkled lip' (why 'wrinkled' exactly? – presumably curled in scorn) and 'sneer of cold command', which suggest to us that the original statue represented a man who was bad-tempered, heartless, cruel. The sculptor seems to have made a special effort to render their qualities. Why? Perhaps just because of his skill? Perhaps also because he had suffered under the cruelty of the king and carried out his work feelingly, as a kind of retribution?

But we have not yet taken in the whole scene. After the broken fragments, the narrator describes to us the pedestal, on which an inscription is still visible. So we learn the name of the figure, 'Ozymandias', and then follow highly significant details about his title and his message to the world. Now to the other qualities associated with him we can add pride ('King of Kings') and a sense of defiance of all other rulers who may have hoped to be compared with him. Why are they bidden to 'despair'? Presumably they can never hope (in Ozymandias' opinion) to equal the magnificence and power symbolized by his mighty statue, which is just one sample of his 'works'.

This is not yet the end of the 'moving picture' we are given, although the rest at first seems mainly negative. 'Nothing beside remains', – and, with what we should now call a cinematographic technique, we are invited to look around, and our eye travels over the empty desert stretching far away into the distance without interruption. If we are reading intelligently, we shall probably ask where *are* all the 'Mighty works' of which Ozymandias seemed so proud? Can it be that they have all disappeared without trace?

By now, we have reached the stage of taking in, fairly fully, the 'situation' and we have seen that the 'development' takes the form chiefly of enlarging the initial picture until certain thoughts begin to form in our mind.

We may be bothered by the question where was all this to be seen? When did Ozymandias rule? What became of his great empire? Was he as bad as the poem suggests? But if we look again, we see that the author makes no attempt to be informative about the historical detail; in fact, on this matter, he gives us no clues to follow up at all, and it seems clear that the interest of the poem is entirely in the character of Ozymandias, in special relation to what has happened in subsequent ages.

Up to this stage we have been doing little more than 'comprehending' the facts given to us in the poem, and we have seen that the relationship between them ... the proud face, the proud inscription ... the fallen statue and the empty desert ... gives us something quite challenging to centre our thoughts upon.

What else? Now we begin to ask what seems to be the writer's intention. What was his main motive, or interest, in giving us this picture? Is he, for example, an admirer of the power of Ozymandias? Is he inviting us to feel melancholy at the thought of the great and powerful king whose empire has crumbled and wasted away? Most readers will feel instinctively that this is not the case. It is interesting to observe that nowhere does the writer dictate an attitude to us, tell us what we ought to think or feel. Unmistakably, however, we feel that the poem is satirical; that Ozymandias is being condemned, and perhaps also mocked, for his foolish presumption in supposing that his power was permanent.

Now that we have sketched out the situation and formed our opinion of the writer's intention, we can read the poem through again to check what we have so far discovered. Then, if we find no reason to change, or correct, our findings, we can begin to fit into the picture a number of the details that we were not fully conscious of, or set on one side, during our preliminary investigation.

What part is played by the 'traveller'? He is there in the first line, as the source of the narrative, but he is soon eliminated, and the poem ends without any more mention of him. He seems to be of little importance, and is just a convenient 'fiction' for introducing us to Ozymandias, of making a 'bridge' between the 'antique' past and the present. Yet the poem does not read entirely like an ordinary traveller's tale; it is factual, certainly, and makes no attempt to impress by exaggeration, but we have an impression that the whole structure of the poem seems more complex than we should expect in an ordinary traveller's tale. For example, the long sentence beginning in line 3 'Near them on the sand' and going on to 'the heart that fed' (line 8) is not easy to grasp in its entirety. We are much inclined to expect a conclusion to the sentence after 'lifeless things' (line 7); so that line 8 takes us by surprise, as we realize that 'survive' is after all a transitive verb. Can we say that line 8, 'the hand that mocked them and the heart that fed' is bothersome and would have been better left out? This is our first reaction, perhaps, but then we see that it causes us to think for a while about the sculptor of the great statue, and we begin to sense a poignant contrast between the great King and his humble employee, who while carving the statue was able to express in silence some of his bitter feelings about the tyrant, who would no doubt have drastically punished any breath of open criticism that might have been made of him. A further poignant thought that may come to us is that the 'and' and the 'heart' that had so feeling a relationship with Ozymandias, and in some ways achieved a kind of superiority over him, have also vanished without either trace or reputation.

Apart from line 8, however, the sense of the whole poem seems to run very naturally, and indeed its whole powerful effect depends on the clear, bold presentation of the situation. Any slight unnaturalness of expression is absorbed quite easily by the strong impact of the subject, and by the well-organized verse form.

If the poem is in some ways propaganda, anti-tyrannical, anti-autocratic propaganda, the writer does not spoil his case by pitching it in too highly coloured or hysterical words. We get the impression that the strong feeling which the poem arouses comes from a cool, reliable observer, whose words command respect. Let us look more closely at the writer's choice of words. The poem opens on a note of extreme bareness.

'I met a traveller from an antique land ...'

'Antique' seems a little out of the ordinary, and we could try the effect of replacing it by 'ancient'; on the whole it seems to make little difference, and the word seems to be placed in a fairly insignificant position. When we come, however, to the sequence 'frown', 'wrinkled lip', 'sneer', 'cold command', we begin to feel that something is being firmly delineated by these sharp, uncompromising words which define the character of Ozymandias so completely, almost as boldly as carvings on stone. Then the adjective 'shattered', with its effect of violent explosion, seems very suitable, and suggests the finality with which not only the king's 'visage' but also his whole empire have been scattered into fragments.

The finest effect in the use of words comes with lines 9 to 12. First, there is a plain, prosaic statement:

And on the pedestal these words appear ...

then suddenly a great trumpet-like burst of sound,

My name is Ozymandias, King of Kings

gaining its effect partly from the magnificent, exotic, multi-syllabic name itself, partly from the 'King of Kings', which is rich in echoes from the barbaric past, as preserved in parts of the Bible, the Prayerbook ('The King's Majesty'), from Handel's *Messiah*. And this is followed up swiftly by the proud, defiant challenge:

Look on *my* works,

(as though everything done during his reign was *his*)

ye Mighty,

(the archaic second person plural adding the touch of ancient fierceness) until the line culminates in the final, terse command, as from a person whose every word is a kind of law,

and despair.

After these two 'magnificent' lines, we are forced, whether in reading aloud or in thought, to pause. Then, in a quietly mischievous way, the narrator goes on to point out, in the simplest possible words:

Nothing beside remains

which seems a damning comment on Ozymandias' pretensions, and the poem ends on a similar note of quiet triumph. The rhythm of the final two-and-a-half lines, in which the sentence unfolds smoothly without break or interruption, seems to convey superbly the effect of the traveller's eye looking up from the shattered fragments, and searching the desert near and far in all directions without seeing another single sign of the 'works' of Ozymandias.

Some other effects in the poem seem worthy of mention. The poem leaves us with a great impression of sculptural compactness. Some of this is due to the verse-form, which we notice is almost that of the sonnet. It is interesting to see that only the first four and the last four lines have a regular rhyming pattern, and the middle section (which caused us some difficulty of comprehension) has not been so completely built in to the general scheme. Nevertheless, we notice how skilfully the writer has set the word groups of his poem into the rhythmic pattern, so that important words are in positions which receive special emphasis.

      Half-sunk .... frown
                      .... command
      Tell   ....

But, in this poem, the device which produces a great deal of the compactness is alliteration. This seems to be used quite unconsciously, and is brought in by the poet's controlled excitement. A certain amount of assonance (vowel correspondence) also contributes to the close-knit harmony. It is seen in line 1 –

    I me*t* a *t*raveller from *an* *an*tique l*an*d

where the 't' and the syllable 'an' each appear three times.
In line 2, the 't' is continued

    Who said '*T*wo vas*t* and *t*runkless legs ...

and the 'st' at the end of line 2 is repeated at the beginning of line 3

    .... *st*one
    *St*and ....

followed by a sequence of 's' and 'sh' sounds

    .... *s*and
    Half-*s*unk a *sh*attered vi*s*age lie*s*, who*s*e frown ...

Soon we are listening to

    *sn*eer of *c*old *c*ommand
    *T*ell that its *s*culp*t*or ...

while line 8 has a special double structure

    The *h*and *that* mocked them, and the *h*eart *that* fed.

The alliteration in '*K*ing of *K*ings' is obvious, and we soon perceive another strong echo in '*M*ighty' of 'Ozy*m*andias'.

Finally in the last line we find *b*oundless and *b*are; co*ll*osa*l*, *l*one and *level* — which all contribute to the impression of forlorn emptiness in the concluding scene.

By now we have examined the poem for most of the factors which make it a powerful and memorable piece of writing. Let us check other points of technique suggested on pages 19–38. Simile, Metaphor? Metaphors appear with the words 'read' and 'stamped', but their contribution is quite a subsidiary one, and obviously this is a poem which depends chiefly on bold plain statements with an element of irony which becomes more marked as the poem develops.

Symbolism? This is the topic which brings us close to an appreciation of the real significance and appeal of the poem. Obviously Ozymandias himself means very little to us or to anyone else in the world today. Nevertheless he, and his undignified end, so vigorously presented in this poem, reminds us of the inevitable fall of all tyrants who ever existed or will exist.

5 The Eye

The Atlantic is a stormy moat, and the Mediterranean,
The blue pool in the old garden,
More than five thousand years has drunk sacrifice
Of ships and blood and shines in the sun; but here the Pacific:
The ships, planes, wars are perfectly irrelevant.
Neither our present blood-feud with the brave dwarfs
Nor any future world-quarrel of westering
And eastering man, the bloody migrations, greed of power, battle-falcons,
Are a mote of dust in the great scale-pan.
Here from this mountain shore, headland beyond stormy headland
    plunging like dolphins through the grey sea-smoke
Into pale sea, look west at the hill of water: it is half the planet
    this dome, this half-globe, this bulging
Eyeball of water, arched over to Asia,
Australia and white Antartica: those are the eyelids that never
    close; this is the staring unsleeping
Eye of the earth, and what it watches is not our wars.

Demonstration

Our search for the basic situation of this poem may leave us for a moment slightly confused. The title is 'The Eye', yet the poem opens by talking about oceans, and then seems to become involved in War. What connection can there be between all these? However, if we retain our wits, it will not take us long to pick up our bearings. In line 4, a good landmark is:

but *here* the Pacific.

and we gain the idea that after some passing allusions to the Atlantic and the Mediterranean, the writer is inviting us to think with him about the Pacific Ocean, near which he is situated as he composes the poem. The key adverb of place 'here' appears again a little later:

Here from this mountain shore ...

and this enables us to picture the poet's situation more precisely: he is standing high up on a mountainous shore, looking out westwards ('look west') across the immensity of the Pacific Ocean, and he is therefore somewhere in America. A further important element in the situation is the presence in the Pacific of the ships and aeroplanes which signify war – though it seems that he does not see these immediately before him but is merely thinking of their presence.

A disconcerting aspect of the opening lines is the grammatical relationship of 'Mediterranean' to the rest, but this uncertainty disappears as soon as we look carefully at the sentence structure and see that, following on the simple sentence:

The Atlantic is a stormy moat,

we have a considerably more complex one, built around the subject 'The Mediterranean' and its two predicates

1) has drunk sacrifice, etc.
2) and shines in the sun.

Now, we can begin to see the nature of the developing thought in the poem. Against the immensity of the Pacific Ocean (and we remember ironically that 'pacific' literally means 'peaceful'), the wars and the blood feuds which take place, whether in the present or the future, seem and will seem, quite trivial and 'irrelevant':

a mote of dust in the great scale-pan.

of very minor significance in the great weighing up of human affairs *sub specie aeternitas*. 'The great scale-pan' a metaphor from weighing, trading and evaluating, is a direct reminder of the Last Judgement, the time when perhaps like Belshazzar in the Book of Daniel, we shall be 'weighed in the balances and found wanting'.

(The word 'mote', not to be confused with 'moat' in line 1, may at first seem unfamiliar, and it is certainly archaic. Nevertheless it occurs in some famous contexts likely to be known to students using this book, such as the line in *Hamlet* referring to the Ghost:

A mote it is to trouble the mind's eye,

or the New Testament parable warning us not to remove 'the mote' that is in our brother's eye, when we ignore the 'beam' which is in our own eye.)

The poet obviously thinks with some disdain, or contempt, of the human warfare which is taking place in the Pacific area. He gives no indication of taking sides, or showing political partisanship, even though as we know he is looking westwards and is presumably an American, or at least American-based. 'Dwarfs' we suspect may refer in a slightly derogatory way to Japanese, or Asian soldiers, but at least they are credited with being 'brave', while

the bloody migrations, greed of power, battle-falcons

refer impartially to 'westering or eastering man'. War certainly exists in the Pacific, and will probably continue to exist, but in the vision of this poet it is no more than a minor, irritating phenomenon, stupid and vicious in itself, but of only ephemeral significance. As his imagination dwells upon the Pacific, it is not the wars which capture his interest, but the sheer immensity of the enormous expanses. We notice that he does not think of it as a vast flat area: his mind has been trained in modern sciences and geography; he is aware that, to astronauts in space 'satellites', the curvature of the Earth's surface is very apparent – we have by now, I expect, all seen photographs to illustrate this. So, we are invited, in a series of metaphors to think of the Pacific as 'a hill of water', a 'dome', a 'half-globe', and by a final, more imaginative act of comparison, 'a bulging eyeball of water'. The comparison, if we think about it, is apt in several ways: in shape, in wateriness, in the division between the outward and the inward parts of the eye, comparable to the watery expanses of the Pacific Ocean contrasted to the landed half of the globe containing Asia and Europe. On the far side of the eyeball-like ocean are Asia, Australia and Antartica which, according to his comparison, represent 'the eye-lids which never close' – because they are too far apart!

The poem does not close merely on this ingenious comparison. Having been given the metaphor of the Pacific as the eye of the Earth, which watches other things than 'our wars', we find ourselves led on to speculate what this 'eye of the world' is watching; and this gives us an impression of the Earth as a sentient, intelligent, watchful being, looking out unblinkingly – into what? No definite answer is given to this question. Into the outer realms of Space, perhaps: into the mysteries and uncertainties of the future. In relation to such immensities, however, how utterly old-fashioned and 'irrelevant' are our quaint out-of-date human activities, such as War.

Now that we have followed the development of the poem in broad outline, we can state its intention more exactly. It is a 'war poem', but its commentary on War is made not by the painting of heart-rending pictures of suffering and death, destruction and agony; nor by extolling the human heroism, the technical skill, the miracles or organization involved. It shows us the phenomena of human warfare against the background of the whole universe, so that we see that War does not belong to the eternal order of things: it is one of the quaintly foolish inventions of mankind, which we may hope they will soon become too mature to indulge in.

Let us now look back through the poem to appreciate other interesting aspects of the writer's technique.

We notice how the first four introductory lines of the poem give us quick passing details of the strife-filled history of the other oceans, and show something of the poet's skill in the choice of metaphor. The Atlantic is not only 'stormy', but long and clearly defined between parallel lines like a 'moat', the military defensive fortification, excavated as it were to protect America against the ravages, 'the greed of power', of Europe. The Mediterranean, though at first glance so beautiful,

> The blue pool in the old garden

'shining in the sun', has for five thousand years, stretching back to the very earliest history of modern man, been living, like a savage, inhuman God, on the sacrifices of ships, men, and 'blood'.

By now, we have certainly noticed that this is not a poem which depends obviously on 'pattern', either of rhyme or the more noticeable kind of rhythm. We do notice, however, that it has a tightness of construction which is based upon an easy, natural flow of normal speech, e.g.

> The ships, planes, wars are perfectly irrelevant ...
> ... look west at the hill of water ...

which is combined with painstaking search for the appropriate word. We notice a careful balancing and continuity of phrasing: the Mediterranean had its sacrifices of 'blood': now, in the twentieth century, it is the Pacific which witnesses the 'blood-feuds'. Wars in the past were limited in scope: any which occur in the future are likely to be no less than 'world-quarrels'. The parties in conflict are not labelled in the usual conventional way as East and West, but 'Eastering' and 'Westering' man: the participial form with its sense of continuous or 'progressive' activity, suggests the perpetually aggressive tendencies of the two rival power-blocks which are always, as it were, quietly on the move towards each other's territories. 'Eastering' and 'Westering' are also recognizable as metaphors from navigation.

A further sudden but bold metaphor is given to us in 'battle-falcons', which are presumably the combat aeroplanes of the warring powers, circling round each other mutually seeking to deliver a death stroke; the particular effect of the metaphor is to distance the aeroplanes from the spectator: we are given no sensational details about the technical refinements of the aircrafts or of the skill and courage of the pilots; they are observed far away and high up, where it is impossible to distinguish friend from foe and where they seem to have the least possible relevance to life on Earth below.

The language of the poem is sparse and economical, but we notice an interesting effect of rhythmic contrast which enters the poem in line 10 and 11. Our thoughts have just been brought back to the actual look-out situation of the poet, and now the words surge out powerfully in long phrases as he creates in our mind a word equivalent of the rhythmic, receding coastline:

> Here from this mountain shore, headland beyond stormy

> headland plunging like dolphins through the grey sea-
> smoke
> Into the pale sea, look west at the hill of water ...

the simile of the 'plunging dolphins' makes a useful contribution to the rythmic sea-scape.

Other neat touches of rhythmic effect occur with the phrase:

> ... this half-globe, this bulging
> *Eyeball* of water ...

where the breaking of the line after 'bulging' throws maximum attention on the very important metaphor 'Eyeball' at the beginning of the following line, and strengthens the power of this unexpected but acceptable conceit. The same effect is repeated two lines later, with the same success:

> ... this is the staring, unsleeping
> Eye of the earth ...

We notice in closing the puzzling, cryptic effect of the final words, given some extra power by the alliterative 'w':

> and *w*hat it *w*atches is not our *w*ars.

*W*hat is it *w*atching if not our *w*ars? we are almost compelled to echo back.

The final judgement on this poem will vary according to the experience of the student-critic. Some sophisticated and widely-read readers may find it to be a rather over-intellectual poem, pretentiously philosophical, and over-derivative from other well-known poems in the English language. On the other hand, it may be expected that, for most students using this book, the poem will stimulate a pleasing and thoughtful use of the intellect and imagination, and will cause them to think about certain problems more carefully than before.

6 In the Cult of the Free

Pass on then, pass on, missile hurled
In your headlong flight to fool the world;
Being self-turned, you never heard
Above our wild herd
And market murmur of assembled waves
A song strange-fallen out of night-caves
Like star all of a sudden from the sky.

I,
Reared here on cow-dung floor,
From antediluvian shore
Heard all, and what good it did!
'Magnificent obsession'
Now magic chords are broken!

Pass on in mad headlong flight
O pass on, your ears right
Full of throttle sound,
So winding up your kaleidoscope
Leave behind unhaunted
An innocent in sleep of the ages.

Demonstration

First, we observe that the poem throughout is cast in the form of an address (an 'Apostrophe') by the writer to someone, or something, using the *second person*:
>... your headlong flight ...
>... your ears ...
>... your kaleidoscope ...

and the principal verbs are in the imperative mood:
>Pass on, ... pass on ...

In order to grasp the situation we have obviously to ask ourselves firstly who is speaking, and secondly *to whom*, or what? Perhaps the second question is easier to begin with. The person or object we read is:
>... missile-hurled
>In headlong flight ...
>... self-turned ...
>... ears right
>Full of throttle sound ...

The answer which suggests itself is that the poem is addressed to the driver of some kind of mechanized vehicle, or possibly to the vehicle itself. What kind of vehicle? The word 'throttle' at first seems to suggest a motor-car, and we can all remember the experience of having to stand aside rather disgustedly, as a fast car goes hurtling past us at full speed, splitting our ear drums and covering us with dust – after which we hurl our curses at the thoughtless driver! Yet this hypothesis does not fit all the facts in the poem particularly well: there is for example, a strong suggestion that the vehicle is not earth-bound, and the idea of:
>headlong flight to fool the world

seems to give the vehicle in question a rather prominent relationship to the rest of the world as a whole, and this line of thought sooner or later brings us to the idea of the 'vehicle' being an artificial 'satellite' – with which everybody in the modern world is now surely familiar. Yes, this hypothesis does fit all the facts we are given:

a satellite is hurled up into space by a rocket, which is very similar indeed to the destructive 'missiles' which we are told the 'great nations' of the world are preparing in case of a future war. The satellite is also 'self-turned': it normally rotates upon itself, which explains why we sometimes observe a winking effect as one of them passes across the night sky. Certainly the typical swift, purposeful passage of a satellite across the sky is well conveyed by the phrase 'headlong flight' – normally a rather hackneyed expression which receives fresh meaning from this new context.

Now, who is speaking? To answer this we do not, of course, need to know exactly who the poet is, what is his name, his nationality, his age, occupation or profession, and so on. From what point of view is he speaking in this particular poem? Into what situation has he in imagination put himself? What evidence can we glean? In the first section of the poem we see a reference to 'our wild herd'; but the second section becomes more definite:

> I
>
> Reared here on cow-dung floor
>
> From antediluvian shore ...

and in the third section:

> An innocent in sleep of the ages.

Also, at this early stage in our study of the poem we have a general sense that the poet is rejecting, or dissociating himself from what he is addressing: he tells it bluntly and repeatedly to 'pass on', as if it had no meaning or interest for him. These facts put together suggest that the poem is written from the point of view of a member of one of the so-called 'developing' countries. He has been reared on a 'floor', – implying a lack of furniture in the European sense; and on a floor on which cow-dung has been mixed to give a finer texture to the mud. The culture which reared him, the writer implies, may have been 'undeveloped' in some senses (few modern buildings, little scientific technology), but it had a long history going back for ages to 'antediluvian' time, i.e. before the pre-historic Flood. This culture had been slow to develop – the writer thinks of it still as enduring through the 'sleep of the ages', but at least it had the virtue of being 'innocent'.

This in general gives us a meaningful idea of the situation: a final touch of precision is given by the details which cause us to picture the writer at the 'shore', the 'antediluvian shore', looking up at the satellite cruising high above, and heading out across the sea, with its market murmurs of assembled waves.

The writer, we note, in spite of his antediluvian origins is very alert, watchful, well aware of the satellite and what it signifies, and his opinions are very definite.

The development of the poem is easily observed. The first of the three sections contains the 'Apostrophe', the invitation to the satellite and the astronaut who pilots it to 'pass on'. The middle section explains who is talking; and the third returns to the theme of the first. In the third, however, we notice a number of slight but significant variations which give us a good clue to the writer's intention. Whereas in section 1 we read:

> Pass on then ... In your headlong flight

in the final section, with the help of an ejaculation and an added epithet, we read:

> Pass on in *mad* headlong flight
> *O* pass on ...

and we can now confirm the impression which has been forming in our mind already, that the writer's intention is to express his disdain or contempt for the satellite, which though 'magnificent' in its skill, power, and precision, represents an element of 'madness': it has become an 'obsession', a craze, which takes hold of a person, or a culture, and occupies such an irresistible position that all sense of balance and proportion is destroyed.

'The magic chords' are broken, the writer tells us: we note that 'chord' here is the musical expression, a collection of sounds which produce harmony; and this may remind us of what we have heard of the 'music of the spheres', the divine music of supernatural beauty, though inaudible to most human ears, which medieval philosophers used to suppose was given out by the revolution of the crystalline spheres upon which the sun, moon, stars, and planets were fixed, as *natural* satellites, around the Earth. Now the magic chords are broken: the writer supposes that he no longer hears the divine music of the 'spheres', and he is disappointed, disillusioned. We begin to recall how so many people, in both developed and developing countries, have been scornful of the great waste of time, energy, brain and money on Space Research. If we look again through the poem, we see this theme appearing at a number of points. The flight of the satellite, we read, is:

> to fool the world,

to deceive the world; to make the world believe that something important is being done when such is not the case. Many thinking people condemn programmes of space research, and projects such as the attempt to put a man on the Moon, for distracting both governments and people from more fundamental tasks such as the elimination of starvation and ignorance, and the establishment of social justice and harmony. The writer has 'heard all' that can be said in support of such scientific projects, and knows 'what good' (i.e., what little, real good) they have so far done. The satellite, we read, is 'self-turned': this has a literal and a metaphoric meaning. It rotates upon itself from the forces imparted to it at the time of its launching; but the astronaut also, like all his directors and employers, is turned in upon himself, i.e. 'self-centred', interested only in his own problems, and quite regardless of the needs and dilemmas of people outside himself. His ears are so full of the 'throttle sound' that he is quite unaware of the sounds, the cries and appeals made by anybody else.

But the astronaut is being condemned (and partly pitied) for something else. Preoccupied with his headlong flight, he misses some other essential things.

> you never heard ...
>
> A song strange-fallen out of night-caves.

What is this strange-fallen song? What does it represent? It relates again to the 'magic chords', the music of the spheres, and thus to all the beauty and the mystery in the universe which materialism and technology so often ignore, and which ironically is often much more vividly perceived and appreciated by the 'innocence', the 'unhaunted', un-obsessed outlook of the less 'civilized' man. So far we have avoided any mention of the title given to this poem, but now we can perhaps see how it and the poem complement each other: the poem is its author's manifesto in 'the cult of the free'. The less technically-developed nations should not be despised or patronized: they have certain essential advantages: they are 'free' from the obsessions of mechanized man. They must understand this, and see that they do not lose their precious 'freedom'. The poem is thus a poem of protest, though we may note that it is not a poem of political protest, and the 'freedom' it celebrates is not just a political 'freedom' from being ruled by an uncongenial and foreign oppressor. The poem is written more at the anthropological level, and is concerned with 'culture contacts', which are both wider and deeper than mere political arrangements. While the poem is something of a protest, it is also something of an appeal: firstly, an appeal to be left in peace; secondly, an appeal to the 'innocents' not to lose, or be seduced from, their heritage.

In what further ways can we strengthen our appreciation of this poem by turning our attention to matters of technique?

First we notice the writer's confident control of language, his easy command of colloquial expression, and especially the emphatic repetitions which give the poem its characteristic manner. Little suggestion here that the English used is only a 'second language', or is other than perfectly natural to the writer:

>   Pass on, then, pass on ...
>   I, reared here on cow-dung floor ...
>   Heard all ...

We have already taken note of the general plan of the poem: now we notice in addition that the structural development, in spite of any difficulty we have had in grasping the theme to begin with, is by means of entirely orthodox English sentences. Only at the end of section two

>   'Magnificent obsession'
>   Now magic chords are broken!

is the thought transition unsupported by firm grammatical coherence, but here as we have seen the ideas can easily enough be fitted into the general theme.

This easy colloquial speech is contained within the line lengths, to give the poem a firm, purposeful movement. Invididual lines are irregular in length and stress pattern, but the poet has made interesting use of rhyming words. Up to the four final lines, the rhymes come in pairs:

>   Hurled; world   heard; herd   waves; caves

In this sequence, we note especially the effect of 'sky' rhyming with the lone one-word line, 'I', at the beginning of the second section: this gives to 'I' an effect of great emphasis, as though to say

> I, on the other hand, in complete contrast ...

As the satellite eventually 'passes on', the rhymes fall away for the last four lines, bringing us memorably to the peaceful close of

> An innocent in sleep of the ages,

in which the 'antediluvian' settles back, after the 'throttle sound' of the passing machine, to his peaceful composure.

The rhyme pattern of the poem is also used to give prominence to some of the poet's happiest phrase-making. 'Missile-hurled' compresses a great deal of meaning into the brief composite past participle rhyming with 'world'. The metaphorical introduction of the market with its cross-talk, its various comings and goings, is a novel way of presenting the sea, while the association of 'caves' with 'night' strengthens the sense of mystery which the astronaut can so easily miss. The abrupt, monosyllabic 'cow-dung floor' which the author uses to symbolize his unsophisticated background makes a sharp contrast with the flowing developed sentence which precedes it. 'A song strange-fallen', with its inversion of normal word order and slight archaism, most aptly suggests the mysterious beauty which escapes the attention of the mechanical man. Thus, in many ways, the poetic skill of the writer has added a good deal of power to this pregnant and visionary poem.

FOOTNOTE In the view of the present writer, the only line of this poem which seems unsuccessful – an ineffective attempt at communication – is

> So winding up your kaleidoscope

The kaleidoscope is an optical instrument, a toy, which produces endless varieties of symmetrical coloured patterns. How can this be made to fit the idea of a satellite is not made clear. Nor is it clear how, either literally, or metaphorically, we can *wind up* a kaleidoscope. It is possible to wind up a watch; we can wind our way up a long meandering road full of diversions. But ...?

Any readers of this book who can 'save' this line from the charge of obscurity are welcome to send their views to the author.

7 The Mountaineers

Despite the drums we were ready to go.
The natives warned us shaking their spears.
Soon we'd look down on them a mile below
rather as Icarus, so many poets ago,
waved to those shy, forlorn ones, dumb on a thumbnail field.
We started easily but oh the climb was slow.

Above us, the red perilous rocks like our pride
rose higher and higher – broken teeth of the mountain –
while below the dizzy cliffs, the tipsy angles signified
breathless vertigo and falling possible suicide.
So we climbed on, ropes constricting our hearts painfully,
our voices babel yet our journey glorified.

The soul too has altitudes and the great birds fly
over. All the summer long we climbed higher,
crag above crag under a copper sulphate sky,
peak above peak singing of the deserted, shy
inconsolable ones. Still we climb to the chandelier stars
and the more we sing the more we die.

So ascending in that high Sinai of the air,
in space and canyons of the spirit, we lost ourselves
amongst the animals of the mountain – the terrible stare
of self meeting itself – and no one would dare
return, descend to that most flat and average world.
Rather, we made a small faith out of a tall despair.
Shakespeare, Milton, Wordsworth, came this way
over the lonely precipice, their faces gold
in the marigold sunset. But they could never stay
under the hurricane tree so climbed to allay

---

line 4 In classical legend Icarus and his father Daedalus escaped from the hostility of King Minos of Crete by means of wings fastened to their bodies.

that voice which cried: 'You may never climb again.'
Our faces too are gold but our feet are clay.

We discovered more than footprints in the snow,
more than mountain ghost, more than desolate glory,
yet now, looking down, we see nothing below
except wind, steaming ice, floating mist – and so
silently, sadly, we follow higher the rare songs of oxygen.
The more we climb the further we have to go.

Demonstration

The opening stanza of the poem corresponds with the title quite easily and we find ourselves following the description of some mountaineers setting out on a long and arduous expedition. This appears to be taking place in a tropical, probably African country: the mountain, we begin to guess, might be Mount Kenya or Kilimanjaro. The 'natives' with their drums and spears try to dissuade, to 'warn' the climbers: perhaps, we may imagine, the mountain is inhabited by gods or spirits which should not be disturbed; perhaps local traditions say that the mountain is unclimbable by human beings. Nevertheless, the climbers start out 'easily' enough, although even in the early stages progress is disappointingly slow. We should notice the verb form 'we'd':

> Soon we'd look down on them a mile below

– soon we *should* look down on them. Already they seem to feel a certain superiority and picture themselves in the position of Icarus, that famous early airman, looking down on those who remain 'earthbound'.

So the poem goes on, developing the description of the typical mountain scenery which the climbers encounter, meeting more and more alarming features as they continue – 'perilous rocks', 'dizzy cliffs' – and we begin to anticipate their final victorious arrival at the summit. Already, however, we should have noticed some details which don't absolutely fit with the idea of a straightforward, practical mountaineering expedition. Also, of course, the journey seems to be endless, and actually there is no mention of a summit or destination. We may be slightly puzzled by the idea of:

> ropes constricting our *hearts* painfully

(Do mountaineers' ropes tend to constrict the 'heart'?), and by:

> our voices babel ...

(Do mountaineers on a long upward climb chatter and shout amongst themselves, in any way resembling Babel?) When we come to the words:

> the soul *too* has altitudes ...

it becomes fairly clear that the poem is about something more than mere mountaineers, and that a parallel of some kind is being suggested with some other aspects of human life. Then, as we come upon the lines:

> Shakespeare, Milton, Wordsworth, came this way
> over the lonely precipice ...

it becomes clear that the 'mountaineers' must be understood to represent *poets*. Not just the three famous ones named, but the whole glorious company' of poets from all over the world, amongst whom the writer seems to include himself. And the mountaineers' upwards climb amongst many perils and difficulties illustrates the aspiring quest of the poet towards some lofty and distant goal. There is no suggestion of what this goal is, and although there are hints of discoveries –

> We discovered *more* than footprints in the snow –

it is not clear what they are, apart perhaps from 'the terrible stare of self meeting itself', which seems to refer to the *painful* dawning of self-knowledge, – painful because it is often a disillusioning process. Whatever the misty objective which the poet/mountaineer pursues, the end is very difficult to achieve. In fact, paradoxically, the nearer they come to it, the further away it seems:

> The more we climb the further we have to go.

Perhaps we should ask ourselves at this point what exactly is the 'intention' of the poem. At first sight it seems a kind of praise song, eulogizing the world-wide company of poets, ancient and modern, for their lofty aims and unswerving endeavour; and a strong impression of this remains to the very end. However, we may not so easily yield our enthusiasm as the author invites us to do; our prosaic, truth-seeking minds may ask such questions as – Can we class all the poets we have known into one group of this kind? Is it true that the greatest poets have not 'dared to descend' to

> that most flat and average world?

Do we want our poets to concern themselves entirely with distant and undefinable aims? Our studies in literature may already have acquainted us with the caustic comment on Shelley, one of the most characteristic English poets of aspiration – that he was like 'a beautiful and ineffectual angel beating in vain his luminous wings in the void' (Arnold: *Essays in Criticism*).

In fact, if we look again at the present poem we shall see that running along together with the praise theme, there is another quieter undercurrent of ironic self-criticism. Up in those lofty 'canyons of the spirit', the author tells us,

> ... we lost ourselves
> amongst the animals of the mountain

thus almost losing their qualities as human beings. Then, although they had still been singing of the 'deserted, shy, inconsolable ones' i.e. those left behind on earth, he tells us

> ... no one would dare
> return,

In this peculiar, unrealistic isolation, the 'mountaineers' had no alternative but to make

> ... a small faith out of a tall despair,

they are being driven on, as if by some kind of compulsion, by the voice which cried

> 'You may never climb again.'

And the same irony is present in the line

> Our faces too are gold but our feet are clay.

We are full of hope and promise, but we achieve little and end by being disappointed. In the end, when the 'mountaineers' look down, searching perhaps for the men of earth, they see nothing below

> except wind, steaming ice, floating mist

and *silently, sadly,* they continue on their endless quest for the enriched experiences ('the songs of oxygen') which they hope to discover.

So much for our initial survey of the 'situation' and 'intention' of the poem. After the more thorough investigation that our examination of the poem's technique involves, we shall have more to say.

A special feature of the technique of the poem is its frequent use of allusions. None of the allusions is more obscure than a person of average education can be expected to recognize and follow up, but all help to place the topic of the poem in a clearer light and in a wider frame of reference. We have commented on the relevance of Icarus, but, especially in view of the ironic undercurrent in the poem, it is worth remembering that Icarus, in spite of his great inventiveness and daring, mounted up so high that the heat of the sun melted the wax used in making his artificial wings; he fell to earth and was killed! Thus Icarus becomes symbolic of the aspirant who overreached himself. A later allusion is to the Tower of Babel, in which the assembled hosts suddenly found themselves talking different languages and unable to understand each other, – perhaps a useful, and certainly *ironic*, reference, to many poets of our own century! Sinai, of course, was the mountain which Moses was commanded to ascend when he was to receive the Commandments from God (*Exodus*, chapter 20); at least *his* mountain climb was fruitful! The phrase 'feet of clay' is also a biblical allusion: not only did the feet of the weary climbers drag as though held back by clay, but like many of the idols worshipped in olden times they were seen to have 'feet of clay', i.e. in spite of their alluring appearance they were seen to be basically of little value.

Another more modern mountaineering saga which is freely alluded to in the later parts of the poem is the series of attempts to climb Everest, the world's highest mountain, in the Himalayas (eventually climbed in 1953). Members of those expeditions have written of the terrifying experiences of doubting one's own identity ('the terrible stare of self meeting itself') which occurs in high and lonely altitudes. There have been stories, too, of the discovery of mysterious footprints in the snow far above the level where any normal forms of life exist, giving rise to legends and speculations about mountain spirits, Abominable Snowmen, and so on. When Everest was finally 'conquered', after many expeditions had failed, it was an expedition which made use of the special stimulant, oxygen gas ('rare songs'). It is also relevant to note that many people questioned the value of Everest expeditions (as we do now the space projects – see Demonstration No. 6), as wasteful of time and energy; nevertheless, the mountaineers of the world were driven on by a restless urge to accomplish this feat, not for any tangible purpose, but just, in the famous words of Sir Edmund Hillary, 'because it was there'.

The language of the poem, we note, is basically very plain with an unusual proportion of plain, plodding monosyllabic words, appropriate to the laborious nature of the journey which is being described. Against this plain background, however, we come across instances of quiet, but carefully thought-out metaphor which adds greatly to the vividness of the basic mountaineering situation. As they ascend, they look back and see the natives 'dumb' – too far away to be heard,
      on a thumbnail field.

We are already familiar with the term, a 'thumbnail sketch', something done hurriedly, roughly, in a small space: here we have the idea of the field on which the natives can still be seen, but not heard, being minutely small. As the climbers continue their progress, the red rocks rise higher – 'like our pride' – human pride, we know, is often very excessive and exaggerated, out of proportion to the realities. The rocky crags of the mountain are compared to 'broken teeth'. The sky becomes clearer and purer as they climb above the clouds until it is '$CuSO_4$ (copper sulphate) blue' – which all amateur chemists will remember for the deep intensity of its blueness. In their onward progress, the stars towards which they aspire are compared metaphorically to 'chandeliers', those hanging group of lamps decorated with much scintillating glass that can be seen hanging from the ceilings of elegant European mansions, or from the roofs of theatres.

Line 25, which we have already quoted, is especially interesting: other great writers we are told came this way over the precipice. It is as though the author himself, after a desperate struggle up to the top of a certain precipice turns and looks back, and seems to ask himself whether it was worth coming all this way at such trouble. In his mind he seems to picture some of his great predecessors, 'Shakespeare, Milton, Wordsworth', coming over the very same edge, their faces gold in the marigold sunset, and his feeling of being associated with some of the great writers of former times gives him renewed courage. The colours mentioned here, incidentally, 'gold' and 'marigold' seem to fit well into the suggestion of an African setting.

In general, the poem unfolds in a calm, even way. The absence of capital letters at the beginning of the lines which do not begin new sentences warns us of its claim to be quite 'prosaic' in manner. Nevertheless, we observe, perhaps with some surprise, that this poem is cast into a regular stanza pattern:

```
a  – go      way
 b – spears  gold
a  – below   stay
a  – go      allay
 c – field   again
a  – slow    clay
```

and this is adhered to systematically throughout. Once we have noticed this we can become aware of its unobtrusive effect of holding each of the stanzas firmly together. The arrangement of rhymes does not give a prominent pattern, and they do not call attention to themselves – evidently the author has chosen his words very carefully and we are never obliged to suppose that he chose an unusual or unsuitable word just because it would fill a gap in his rhyme scheme. One of the chief effects of the rhyme scheme employed here is to throw a quiet emphasis on the final lines of each section, and this is particularly notable in the very last line of the poem.

The more we have to climb, the further we have to go.

In 'The Mountaineers', then, we find an ingenious weaving together of themes. Firstly, as the basis of the allegory, there is the endless climb among the high and fearful mountains. Then, as we translate this into broader terms, we are given an impression of the unquenchable aspirations of the world's poets, among whom the writer includes himself. Running along with this, we notice a typical twentieth-century self-consciousness when the poet, in another part of his mind, reflects with a certain nostalgia on the insubstantial nature of his quest. Perhaps our conclusion about the poem could be that it is neither entirely a praise poem, nor entirely a satirical poem, but that its intention is to record the tensions which develop in the mind of the poet between the claims of his visions and the claims of ordinary, 'average' life.

8   Hawk Roosting

I sit in the top of the wood, my eyes closed.
Inaction, no falsifying dream
Between my hooked head and hooked feet:
Or in sleep rehearse perfect kills and eat.

The convenience of the high trees!
The air's buoyancy and the sun's ray
Are of advantage to me;
And the earth's face upward for my inspection.

My feet are locked upon the rough bark.
It took the whole of Creation
To produce my foot, my each feather:
Now I hold Creation in my foot.

Or fly up, and revolve it all slowly –
I kill where I please because it is all mine.
There is no sophistry in my body:
My manners are tearing off heads –

The allotment of death.
For the one path of my flight is direct
Through the bones of the living.
No arguments assert my right:

The sun is behind me.
Nothing has changed since I began.
My eye has permitted no change.
I am going to keep things like this.

Demonstration

Our first reading of this poem again leaves us with a slight sense of bewilderment, in that it presents us with something not immediately and completely coherent, something different from anything we have met before. The title guides us a little at first. 'Hawk Roosting' – hawk, a bird of prey, we think: 'roosting' (related to 'resting'): the taking up of a position on a tree or other high object by a bird during the night, or when not otherwise engaged. As we read the poem through, perhaps several times, we notice the series of short abrupt statements of which it is composed, and we see also that they all involve forms of the 'first person' (I, my, me, mine). If our imagination is reasonably flexible, it does not take us long to see that the words of the poem represent the thoughts, in a kind of internal monologue, which the writer supposes to be running through the mind of the hawk. Whether our knowledge of hawks is based on our personal observations, on pictures in books, on captive specimens in zoos, or from examples seen in films or television programmes, we are reminded by the poem that the hawk always gives an impression of being a fierce, cruel, arrogant creature. The poem conveys to us an unmistakable picture of the hawk through a few characteristic details – 'hooked head ... hooked feet', but it goes further than this and gives us a vivid impression of the spirit, or character of the hawk – of the particular manifestation of the life-force that is seen in it. In the background of our mind now arise all the animal fables we have come across in our lives (they occur in the traditional literature of every culture in the world), in which animals are given individual characters, are able to speak like human beings, and which are often used to convey some kind of moral lesson. In this poem, we observe, no inverted commas, or 'speech marks' are used, and there is no narrative introduction – indeed not even a 'story' of any kind. Our attention is concentrated on the hawk itself, characteristically perched on the highest tree in the wood, or forest; and we are asked to follow a sequence of thoughts and opinions which, according to the writer's imagination, are passing through its mind.

Is this just an 'animal poem', of the kind that would appear in an anthology under the title of 'BIRDS and BEASTS'? Quite quickly, I think, we get an impression that there is more to the poem than that. As we begin to investigate the *development*, and to glimpse the *intention*, we begin to see that here too, as in other traditional animal fables, there is an underlying meaning. The poem certainly begins with the perceptive presentation of just a 'hawk roosting', but it goes much beyond that, and we soon understand that, as has happened to so many birds in literature (cocks, hens, geese, swallows, ostriches, frigate-birds, albatrosses, weavers, and nightingales), the hawk is offered as a symbol. But of what?

Nowhere has the writer stated his intention openly; certainly he affixes no obvious moral or proverb, from which we can grasp his intention without the need for any real thought. He has obviously been writing for fairly sophisticated readers, and I think the significance gradually grows as we read the poem over thoughtfully, until it becomes something of a certainty by the final line.

From the very first line we have an impression of the economical, sparing nature of the language used:
> I sit in the top of the wood, my eyes closed

This is followed bluntly by the single word
> Inaction

which starkly, without the aid of a completed sentence, tells us of the absolute immobility of the hawk, as though deeply involved in inward thoughts. Then we follow the hawk's reflection that, although it is motionless, it is certainly not 'dreaming': no fantasies, visions, speculations or ideals occur in its mind to interrupt the complete coordination between its 'hooked head' and its 'hooked feet', between the brain which thinks and the feet which act. If anything takes place at all, it is the 'rehearsal', the mental repetition of 'perfect kills'. This suggests, rather gloatingly, the swift, sudden, unerring way in which a hawk will swoop down on its prey and carry it off to eat on its lofty perch. The hawk's pride seems to expand in the second stanza: it is obviously pleased with itself, unafflicted by doubts, hesitations or fears, and expresses itself in an almost arrogant way. The high trees (on which it depends) seem to be there for its own, exclusive convenience; the air, with its supporting buoyancy, on which it rides and soars, the warmth and light of the sun, similarly seem to exist solely for its 'advantage'. The whole earth spread out below, as the hawk flies or sits on his lofty perch, seems to him to be offering itself submissively for 'inspection', as a slave or soldier might submit to inspection by his master or commander. His hooked feet, which are tightly 'locked' upon the branch, seem in his thoughts to signify the complete power, the absolute power, he feels over the whole Creation – as he understands it. And in his mind arises the idea that the whole Creation, the whole universe, with its long painstaking process of evolution, has had no other purpose than to produce him – that he is the final culmination, or triumph, of the whole of existence. Now that Creation has evolved him, he in his turn has asserted his power, and assumed control of the processes which have produced him. The passing attention given to the details – 'my foot, my each feather' – conveys the vivid intensity with which the hawk seems conscious of every single element in its make up.

If he chooses to 'fly up', he goes on to think, the whole world seems to revolve according to his own movements. (Those who have travelled in an aeroplane will remember the illusion of the earth appearing to tip up or down, or to swing round, as the pilots operate the controls, and there is no sense that it is the observer in flight who is changing *his* position.) As he flies along, he remembers how he looks for a chance to kill wherever he sees a suitable opportunity; and this, in his self-centred mind, makes him feel like a tyrant with unrestricted power over his subjects, who can act as he pleases without permission, remorse or pity 'because it is all mine'. His nature is entirely physical and natural; in his body, he thinks, there is 'no sophistry', no discussion, no deliberation, no 'dispute of what is fit and not', no questioning of the truth or the justice of any action. His 'manners' – ('manners' of course, are habits and customs generally observed by whole communities, and usually imply refinement, 'civilization', consideration for other people) – *his* habits go no further than the ruthless 'tearing off heads', the 'allotment' – the dealing out of death. His existence flourishes upon 'the bones of the living'. His 'right' – to do as he pleases – is not based on any argument, or any form of legality, which could be discussed and therefore perhaps challenged – it is *absolute*. '*L'etat c'est moi*' (*The State is myself*) in the words of Louis XIV, *le roi soleil*, 'the sun king', the absolute monarch of pre-revolutionary France in the early eighteenth century.

At some point, our minds will by now have made the transition from bird life to human life, upon which the poem depends, and which unlocks its symbolism. While we shall continue to recognize that each of the statements or sentiments attributed to the hawk do match its physical, hawk-like qualities, the real topic of the poem has broadened out, and what we are considering is the extension of the hawk into human affairs, whether in history or in the contemporary world. We find we are thinking about the phenomenon of powerful, ruthless, deadly physical force, unsupported by any kind of legality or morality, and devoid of any mercy, humanity, or humility. Of such power the hawk is a perfect symbol – and we recall how many of the mighty rulers, the great tyrants of history, have adopted birds of prey (the eagle, the falcon) or beasts of prey (the lion, the leopard, the wolf) as their personal emblems.

As we read through to the end of the poem, each additional detail confirms this interpretation. The sun is 'behind' the hawk, both literally as he searches the earth for prey, and also in his mind symbolically, in the sense that the sun, the great source and preserver of life, helps to maintain and guarantee his power. His eye, severe, unflinching – the imperious all-seeing eye of the bird of prey – 'permits', as he supposes, 'no change': no evolution of institutions, no reforms, no improvement, no challenge to his authority. The final line of the poem proclaims, without any doubt, his satisfaction with the *status quo*, with the existing system, and his determination to 'keep things like this'. There is no need for us to mention names, but anyone acquainted with world affairs can think of any number of people (whether Kings, Presidents, Dictators, or Prime Ministers) whose attitude to their subjects and their communities is neatly and sharply condemned in this poem. Perhaps too, on a smaller scale, every lesser human community will provide examples of the same autocratic tendency.

There is, however, still more to this poem, and at a deeper level it is condemning more than individual tyrants. Certain allusions and references justify us in assuming that the ultimate aim of the poet's attack is Man himself; and that the hawk is typical of at least some tendencies of the human race as a whole. We know with what pride we like to think of Man, *homo sapiens*, as the highest creature in the scale of evolution: our deepest myths and legends express this, for example, the Biblical story of creation reserving Man for the sixth day; and indeed there is little doubt that all the facts of history and of science support this view. And as time goes on, the view seems to become more and more plausible; as modern man forges ahead, extending his scientific and technological powers, eliminating a disease here, synthesizing a new form of life there; restoring fertility to deserts, throwing his satellites out ever deeper into space, there is a great tendency for men to adopt the view that they do in fact 'hold Creation' in their grasp. To many thoughtful people, however – some with a religious point of view, some with a purely humanistic philosophy – this seems a thoroughly misguided and conceited, let alone a blasphemous, view. The ancient Greeks in their tragedies made frequent use of the idea of the chastisement of 'hubris', the disaster and punishment which befell men of excessive pride. Certainly a more sober look around the world with its problems of cynicism, superstition, intolerance, war, racial strife, mental disease, suicide and trivial aimless living should be a salutary check to any human being inclined to be too pleased with the progress of the human race; and he may realize that far more difficult problems confront the human race than can be solved by the 'manners' of the hawk, determined merely 'to keep things like this'.

We can say therefore that this poem, by presenting a grimly horrifying picture of insensitive and arrogant power, makes an urgent plea for the preservation of civilized values in human affairs.

'Hawk Roosting' is a poem in which 'meaning' and 'technique' are so closely interwoven that they can hardly be separated, and many of the more usual matters for commentary and 'appreciation' hardly seem to arise. If we search the poem for more formal, recognizable aspects of technique, we observe that it has no regular metre, no rhyming pattern (apart from 'feet'/'eat'); few unusual words suggesting a resourceful vocabulary: no ingenious simile or metaphors. Yet the poem certainly gives us a great impression of compactness, organization and force. How is this achieved?

The poem has an irregular line-by-line structure: the lines are of unequal length, with no regular stresses apart from those given by the normal speech stresses, but each one seems to contain a significant new slab of meaning to add to what has gone before, and the mental effort needed to assimilate each line to what has gone before gives the poem a slow, weighty movement. The grouping of four lines at a time into a very plain stanza form again contributes to the steady, measured growth of the ideas of the poem, and one may sense a remorseless rhythmic effect in the poem as a whole, which is the dramatic counterpart of the heavy, resistant mind of the hawk, and of what the hawk symbolizes.

The choice of words is also interesting. While no single word or expression is unusual or far-fetched, the poem is not 'easy' to read: it just cannot be read quickly or lightly. Partly this is because the writer seems deliberately to have avoided any of the usual 'word-grease', the familiar collocations, the quickly recognized word groups which help us smoothly to enter into a situation (e.g. Ladies and Gentlemen!, Once upon a time!, This is the story of ...). Every single word needs careful evaluation in its context, just as much by a native English speaker as by a second-language student. It is also due to the fact that so many of the expressions from which the writer has built up the poem have a strong ironic element in them, i.e. they invite us to interpret them at two levels of significance. The apparently simple, colloquial phrases which aptly fit the rather unsophisticated mind of the hawk,

> ... the convenience of the high trees!
> ... of advantage to me ...
> ... it is all mine
> ... the sun is behind me
> ... I am going to keep things like this

also expresses its colossal, self-centred impertinence; and the process of following up the two layers of meaning again prevents us from rushing through the poem in a superficial way.

Just imagine how much would be missed by a reader who did not respond to the ironical double meaning of the poem: it would seem a rather rough, ugly, ineffective piece of writing. In fact, this seems to be one of the subtlest, and yet most powerful poems of the century.

9 A Polished Performance

Citizens of the polished capital
Sigh for the towns up-country,
And their innocent simplicity.

People in the towns up-country
Applaud the unpolished innocence
Of the distant villages.

Dwellers in the distant villages
Speak of a simple unspoilt girl,
Living alone, deep in the bush.

Deep in the bush we found her,
Large and innocent of eye,
Among gentle gibbons and mountain ferns.

Perfect for the part, perfect,
Except for the dropsy
Which comes from polished rice.

In the capital our film is much admired,
Its gentle gibbons and mountain ferns,
Unspoilt, unpolished, large and innocent of eye.

Demonstration

The situation in the poem is more complex than those we have already examined, and the title does not at first give a very clear indication of what we are to expect. The poem is exceptionally simple in its elements, but does not fit into any of the more familiar patterns of English poetry, and, therefore, calls for careful consideration. We need to read it over several times, pondering how the different details in the situation are presented to us or referred to, looking for a clue which shows how the whole poem fits together.

The poem opens with a reference to the 'citizens of the polished capital', which suggests the inhabitants of the large, sophisticated, modernized, commercialized city, who 'sigh' or long for, or wish themselves to be back in some of the 'towns up-country', more modest places where (they like to think) life is less difficult, freer from the complications and frustrations connected with such things perhaps as housing, unemployment, cost of living, and conflicting moral standards. In the second stanza we are reminded that even in the 'towns up-country' the people are by no means satisfied with the conditions of their existence, and tend to think with admiration and envy of the simple, 'unpolished', innocence of the village people who live, free from the strains of modern life, still further from the polished capital. Yet, in stanza three, if we journey to the distant villages, we find that the people there do not think of their condition as in any way perfect or enviable, and tell us that if we want to find a simple, unspoilt girl we should look for her right away from the village, 'deep in the bush'.

We notice two things about the way the poem has developed so far. It is obviously based to some extent on the idea that human beings are never satisfied: they always wish themselves in circumstances which they hope will be better than the ones they are actually in. If by some chance they find themselves moved into these other circumstances, they soon realize that they are not fully satisfied with these either, and begin to imagine again some other set of circumstances which is *really* what they want – and so the process of 'wishful-thinking', with which we are all familiar, can go on. (In some developing countries, of course, the process of wishful-thinking at present operates in the reverse direction: the rural farmer (or his son) thinks he will be better off in the village, the villager in the town, and the townsman joins in the mad rush to the capital city – often, of course, to be severely disillusioned. Our present poem, however, is written from the point of view of the 'citizen of the polished capital' who, having experienced the emptiness of the excitement and pleasure of the affluent city, begins to long for something simpler.)

The second thing we notice as we read through the first three stanzas is a gradual transition from the general to the particular. The first two stanzas seem to be presenting the general tendency of people who wish to be somewhere other than where they are; but in stanza three, we observe the suggestion of a search for a particular individual – a girl who is 'simple, unspoilt', representing perhaps the ideal type that the nation, or the race, can produce.

This development of thought becomes clearer when we come to stanza four and notice that the tense of the verb changes suddenly from the habitual present to the historic past.

Deep in the bush we *found* her,

and we are now compelled to think of a particular group of people ('we') engaged at a definite point of time in a search for a definite individual. And it appears, to begin with, that their search has been successful. There she was

Large and innocent of eye,

in a setting, too, which seemed to be all that the searchers had hoped for: none of the filth, turmoil, ugliness of the great city, but

Amid gentle gibbons and mountain ferns.

We notice that no great wealth of descriptive adjectives is used here, but the brief touches of 'gentle gibbons' and 'mountain ferns' suggest something of a beautiful, paradise-like background. The searchers seem to be very pleased with their discovery. There she was

Perfect for the part, perfect.

For the moment we do not think so much about the 'part' which the girl has to play, as about the repetition of 'Perfect ... perfect', a use of language which suggests the admiring satisfaction of the searchers. The second 'perfect' seems to lead us to a pause, as though the

searchers in their complete satisfaction have been left speechless –
but then comes the sinister word 'Except', and we realize that the
supposed perfection is in fact once again marred by imperfection.
In this case the simple unspoilt girl, living deep in the bush, presents
the symptoms of dropsy. We guess at once that this is some kind of
deformity: our knowledge of tropical diseases may be enough to
remind us that 'dropsy', the abnormal swelling of the limbs and
the body, is one of the chief symptoms of beri-beri, the deficiency
disease which in fact comes from eating 'polished rice': rice which,
significantly for our poem, in order to give it a more pleasing appearance, has had all its natural goodness 'polished' away.

What a sudden irony arises here! The girl lives an unsophisticated, unpolished existence; close to that, we might say, for which
she was created – ideal in so many ways: yet, we discover this simple
unspoilt existence has its cost. It is associated with poverty, restricted living conditions, unvaried diet, ignorance. The poem does
not, of course, specify these in details, but they all are suggested to
us by the general context of ideas which all educated people associate
with 'dropsy' and 'polished rice'. Once more, we realize the search
for the ideal has been betrayed.

But now at the beginning of stanza six, we find ourselves being
given further information, which sets the whole poem in a different
perspective. The key-line is

In the capital our film is much admired,

and we now understand that the 'we' of line 10 refers not only to the
sophisticated 'citizens of the polished capital' in general, but more
precisely to a group of film makers. The tense of the verb has
switched significantly again to the immediate present, and we are
told that the film they have made *is* being much admired. Now we
realize that the 'unpolished' girl they were searching for was needed
to play a 'part', a certain role in their film. We are given no hint of
exactly what kind of film it was – whether the dramatization of a
famous novel, or a documentary film on the life of the people of the
country: this does not seem relevant to the poet's intention.

Have we yet come to the climax of the poem? Have we yet discovered the writer's chief intention? I think this is found only in a
careful consideration of the two final lines. We soon notice that these
a rerepetition of phrases occurring earlier in the poem, and seem at

first to have the effect of a gentle recapitulation intended to bring the poem quietly to a close. But if we insist on observing the strict grammatical construction of the final stanza, we notice that these phrases which were applied earlier on to the girl and her setting are now applied to the film itself:

Its gentle gibbons and mountain ferns,
Unspoilt, unpolished, large and innocent of eye

and we may sense a special purpose in the repetition of these phrases in a slightly different context. The significant point is, surely, that the unpleasant facts about the simple unspoilt girl (her 'dropsy' and all that it signifies) do not appear in this final list, and we therefore presume have been omitted in the film. Films, as we ought to be aware, do not always present the whole truth about a situation, but a pleasant, 'glossy' or idealized version, with the unpleasant facts conveniently overlooked: and of course this applies equally to the 'entertainment' as well as the 'documentary' type of films. In our poem the film has been 'unspoilt' by any reference to the girl's dropsy: it is 'large and innocent of eye' – it does not look closely or critically at the situation it presents to us.

We have now surveyed in some detail the poem's situation, the nature of its development, and in so doing have been compelled to consider the writer's aim, or intentions. The poem, as we have seen, has several layers of meaning. Basically it refers to the contrast between the different ways and standards of city life and rural life, but it is chiefly concerned to point out a number of human failings or weaknesses. We have already noticed the reference to the general tendency always to imagine that life is better 'elsewhere'. In addition to this, we should notice the writer's satirical *glance* (not an outright *attack*) at the common belief (inherited particularly from the English Romantic poets of the early nineteenth century) that the finest way of life is found far from the 'din of towns and cities', and in closest contact with the world of 'Nature', especially if there are some mountains in the background! These problems we have seen, are, given a special focus through the search by some film makers for the right type of girl to appear in their film; and we are thus reminded of the common habit of film makers (and perhaps of writers and artists generally) of avoiding the whole truth and presenting to the public whatever is most pleasing or convenient. (There is of course, a branch of literature nowadays, and indeed of film-making, which concentrates on showing us the sordid details of life and nothing else; and of course, that kind of literature and film-making is just as false and far from the truth as the over-sentimental, romanticized one.) The poem is thus ultimately a homily on artistic integrity.

What else is there to say about the technique employed in this poem? It manages without many of the more common devices used by poets; it makes no use of rhyme, regular metrical pattern; it contains no startling metaphor or simile; its epithets are sparse, its rhythm unspectacular; a few touches of alliteration may perhaps be observed (citizens ... capital; gentle gibbons) but these have only a very slight effect. We have to say that this is almost entirely a poem of statements. Grammatically it consists of five quite simple sentences, none with any great elaboration of syntax or mood. The important thing in the appreciation of the poem is to be able calmly to apprehend the separate statements of the poem as they are made, see how they fit together, and to be able to infer the conclusions that they suggest.

An important thing to realize is that the poem is not much concerned with verbal music or finery, but depends very much on the subtleties of the speaking voice, and as we read it we seem to hear the plain, deliberate, ironic voice of the narrator. Is it then a poem at all? Yes, because we are strongly aware of the highly selected, controlled use of language by which it has been built up; and we soon begin to appreciate that there is a definite underlying pattern of construction. We observe the measured regularity of the opening lines of each stanza:

> Citizens of the polished capital ...
> People of the towns up-country ...
> Dwellers in the distant villages ...

there is certainly no metrical regularity here; although we may have a sense of three principal stresses in most of the lines, this is not invariable; some have two, some have four. By the very sparseness of his language, the writer forces our attention on to the individual words and encourages us to weigh up their meanings and their secondary meanings. In particular, the poem centres round the different implications of the words 'polished' and 'unpolished', and, as we have seen, we can learn a great deal from thinking about the various meanings which these bear. How really important is 'polish'?

There is no doubt that this rather dry, undemonstrative poem has a good deal to say to us. It is quite important to become accustomed to this style of poem, which is close to the most basic functions of language. Examples occur in the very earliest literature written in English, and this manner of writing is frequently used by poets using the English language today, when its economical, controlled expression is more in accord with the 'climate' of the twentieth century, its stream-lined aeroplanes, sky-scrapers, and ferro-concrete bridges, than the colourful rhetoric of other ages.

10 Bori

I sat on my bed and tried to think, with my head in my hands. But a huge sledgehammer was beating down on my brain as on an anvil and my thoughts were scattering sparks. I soon realized that what was needed was action; quick, sharp action. I rose to my feet and willed myself about gathering my things into the suitcase. I had no clear idea what I would do next, but for the moment that did not trouble me; the present loomed so large. I brought down my clothes one at a time from the wardrobe, folded them and packed them neatly; then I brought my things from the bathroom and put them away. These simple operations must have taken me a long time to complete. In all that time I did not think anything particularly. I just bit my lower lip until it was sore. Occasionally words like 'Good Heavens' escaped me and came aloud. When I had finished packing, I slumped down in the chair and then got up again and went out into the sitting-room to see if the sounds were still coming. But all was now dark and quiet upstairs. 'My word!' I remember saying; then I went to wait for Elsie. For I knew she would come down shedding tears of shame and I would kick her out and bang the door on her for ever. I waited and waited, and then, strange as it may sound, dozed off. When I started awake I had that dull heavy terror of knowing that something terrible had happened without immediately remembering what it was. Of course, the uncertainty only lasted one second, or less. Recollection and pain followed soon enough, and then the humiliating wound came alive again and began to burn more fresh than when first inflicted. My watch said a few minutes past four. And Elsie had not come. My eyes misted, a thing that had not happened to me in God knows how long. Anyway the tears hung back. I took off my pyjamas, got into other clothes, and left the room by the private door.

I walked for hours, keeping to the well-lit streets. The dew settled on my head and helped to numb my feelings. Soon my nose began to run and, as I hadn't brought a handkerchief, I blew it into the roadside drain by closing each nostril in turn with my first finger. As dawn came, my head began to clear a little and I saw Bori stirring. I met a night-soil man carying his bucket of ordure on top of a battered felt hat drawn down to hood his upper face while his nose and mouth were masked with a piece of black cloth like a gangster. I saw beggars sleeping under the eaves of luxurious department stores and a lunatic sitting wide awake by the basket of garbage he called his possession. The first red buses running empty passed me and I watched the street lights go off finally around six. I drank in all these details with the early morning air. It was strange perhaps that a man who had so much on his mind should find time to pay attention to these small inconsequential things; it was like the man in the proverb who was carrying the carcass of an elephant on his head and searching with his toe for a grasshopper. But that was now it happened. It seems that no thought – no matter how great – had the power to exclude all others.

Demonstration

The passage obviously comes from a novel or story. We cannot deduce a great deal of the general situation in which it occurs, but the passage itself is quite self-contained. We can recognize that it concerns a person who has recently suffered from some kind of stupefying shock, apparently connected with the non-appearance of a girl called Elsie. To begin with he is presented to us in a bedroom, perhaps in a hotel or private house, where he is a visitor. As a result of the shock he has experienced, he is preparing to leave. He falls asleep for a short time, wakes up suddenly, and decides to go. In the hours before dawn he wanders round the streets of a large city, Bori, which seems to be characterized by extremes of modern luxury and sordid poverty. The carrying of the 'night-soil' through the streets of the well-lit city, as well as some other aspects of the writing which we shall examine later, suggests that Bori is a great city in one of the developing countries.

There is little to hinder our rapid assimilation of the passage: in fact all the resources of technique are used to assist our progress. It is not spectacularly 'literary', with quantities of original or ingenious figurative devices, or learned allusions. All the same, it has a definite character of its own, and we can find plenty to say about the means used to create its effects.

The basic language of the passage is very simple and unpretentious. If we resolve this into the two elements of sentence formation and vocabulary, we notice the easy variation of the sentence pattern. Of course, as we read the passage spontaneously we do not take conscious thought of them, because our thoughts are held principally by the sense, the narrative. But when we do come to look consciously at the sentence formation, we notice the variations in length, and word order: here, for example are five consecutive sentences:

i   I brought down my clothes one at a time from the wardrobe, folded them, and packed them neatly; then I brought my things from the bathroom and put them away.

ii   These simple operations must have taken me a long time to complete.

iii   In all that time I did not think anything particularly.

iv   I just bit my lower lip until it was sore.
v   Occasionally words like 'Good Heavens' escaped me, and came out aloud.

The effortless, unmarked progress of the sentences here seems a perfect reflection of the rather entranced, dreamy state of mind of the narrator.

The vocabulary is also restrained. Possibly the word 'ordure' is the only slightly incomprehensible word, but it is difficult to think of an acceptable alternative for that context. At moments when deliberate intensification is needed, however, we find a sharp, emphatic repetition:

action; quick, sharp action

or a vivid phrase such as

I started awake

which is much more dramatic than 'I woke up'; and

I slumped down into the chair.

The general manner of the passage keeps very close to colloquial speech, which is obviously most appropriate to the intimate first-person narrative. Not surprisingly, therefore, the language moves quite easily from the 'colloquial' to the 'slangy'. Slang, we know, is often condemned by schoolmasters, but we know that it often provides a more vigorous way of expressing our thoughts. For example:

I would *kick her out* and bang the door on her for ever
... a thing that had not happened in God knows how long

Some readers might be inclined to condemn what they would call the blasphemous use of the name of God here (see the Second Commandment) but its use in the context can be justified as it is just the kind of loose expression that people, in situations such as that of the narrator, do in fact use.

The writer is by no means incapable of metaphor, as we see from the very effective introduction of the 'sledgehammer beating down on my brain', which continues logically to the comparison of his 'thoughts' to 'scattering sparks'; the comparison of his shock to a 'wound'; and of the night-soil man to a 'hooded gangster'. It seems right, however, that such colouring should be used fairly sparingly, so that nothing can come between the reader and the dull, stark facts of the narrative.

The facts presented in the passage, in themselves, have little importance; and indeed the writer's chief intention is to convey to us the desperate but inarticulate *feelings* of the narrator. His shock (whatever was its cause) has been so great, perhaps so unexpected, that he is still suffering from a kind of mental concussion, and cannot organize or express his thoughts with any exactness. All his mind seems able to do is to register, to photograph, the factual phenomena which come before him. There is no apparent selection of facts to give either a favourable or an unfavourable impression: everything is seen with complete objectivity. The narrator bites his lower lip until it is sore! The dew settles on his head. He blows his nose 'into the roadside drain by closing each nostril in turn with my first finger'. He meets the night-soil man 'carrying his bucket of ordure'. He sees beggars; 'the first red buses running empty'. In fact, of course, this stream of 'small inconsequential things' (in the narrator's own words) is highly effective. The stream of dull, unglamorous detail serves as a very effective symbol, a good example of the 'objective correlative' (see page 8) of the state of mind which the author is conveying to us. How effectively sordid and sinister are some of these objective facts: the writer's talent for blunt realism with a very faint undertone of irony, is well illustrated by the details of the night-soil man, carrying his bucket by head-carriage

> on top of a battered felt hat drawn down to hood his upper face while his nose and mouth were masked with a piece of black cloth

and even more so by the description of the beggars

> sleeping under the eaves of luxurious department stores

and the lunatic

> sitting wide-awake by the basket of garbage he called his possession.

Towards the end of the passage a distinct difference of technique is used, and this, working retrospectively, has the effect of charging with significance the plain facts which have occupied our attention previously. The thought, instead of being concerned with isolated facts plainly presented, becomes more generalized, and this particular scene becomes linked up with other areas of human experience of a similar kind. This collective experience appears, of course, in the form of the proverb which is quoted. Not one of these utterly dead and hackneyed proverbs of the English language (e.g. Too many cooks spoil the broth; Neither a borrower nor a lender be), but one which strikes an English speaker as fresh and vivid, obviously contributed to the language from a different folklore. And while linking up the narrator's experience with that of many other sufferers, the proverb in itself also gives us a very effective symbol of his state of mind:

> It was like the man in the proverb who was carrying the carcass of an elephant on his head and searching with his toe for a grasshopper.

The element of incredibility in the proverb, of a man carrying the carcass of an elephant on his head is made the more acceptable by the exact detail of his '*searching with his toe* for a grasshopper'. The credit for creating the proverb ought to go in the first place to the collective consciousness of the people who created it. But at least we can give some credit also to our author for remembering it and bringing it in a very suitable moment!

Again, in case we are inclined to be sceptical of the facts narrated, to find them 'strange', the writer gives us a simple and sincere assurance:

> that was how it happened.

And the final sentence with its generalization –

> no thoughts – no matter how great – had the power to exclude all others.

also has a reassuring effect: the writer is not just 'a camera': he has a sober reflective mind, and he knows exactly what he is doing.

Our examination of the passage will remind us that even the most apparently straightforward and simple piece of writing may conceal considerable delicacies of technique if we patiently look for them.

(How many readers of the passage, observing the sentence 'I walked for hours' have checked on the time-references in it and discovered the apparent exaggeration in 'hours'. If any have, they should consider whether this is just an 'inconsistency', or whether it has a legitimate artistic purpose.)

11 The Eye

The eye-ball is a little camera. Its smallness is part of its perfection. A spheroid camera. There are not many anatomical organs where exact shape counts for so much as with the eye. Light which will enter the eye will traverse a lens placed in the right position there. Will traverse; all this making of the eye which will see in the light is carried out in the dark. It is a preparing in darkness for use in light. The lens required is biconvex and to be shaped truly enough to focus its pencil of light at the particular distance of the sheet of photosensitive cells at the back, the retina. The biconvex lens is made of cells, like those of the skin but modified to be glass-clear. It is delicately slung with accurate centring across the path of light which will in due time, some months later, enter the eye. In front of it a circular screen controls, like the iris-stop of a camera or microscope, the width of the beam and is adjustable, so that in a poor light more is taken for the image. In microscope, or photographic camera, this adjustment is made by the observer working the instrument. In the eye this adjustment is automatic, worked by the image itself!

The lens and screen cut the chamber of the eye into a front half and a back half, both filled with clear humour, practically water, kept under a certain pressure maintaining the eye-ball's right shape. The front chamber is completed by a layer of skin specialized to be glass-clear, and free from blood-vessels which if present would with their blood throw shadows within the eye. This living glass-clear sheet is covered with a layer of tear-water constantly renewed. This tear-water has the special chemical power of killing germs which might inflame the eye. This glass-clear bit of skin has only one of the fourfold set of skin-senses; its touch is always 'pain', for it should not be touched. The skin above and below this window grows into movable flaps, dry outside like ordinary skin, but moist inside so as to wipe the window clean every minute or so from any specks of dust, by painting over it fresh tear-water.

The light-sensitive screen at the back is the key structure. It registers a continually changing picture. It receives, takes, and records a moving picture life-long without change of 'plate', through every waking day. It signals its shifting exposures to the brain.

This camera also focuses itself automatically, according to the distance of the picture interesting it. It makes its lens 'stronger' or 'weaker' as required. This camera also turns itself in the direction of the view required. It is moreover contrived as though with forethought of self-preservation. Should danger threaten, in a moment its skin shutters close, protecting its transparent window. And the whole structure, with its prescience and all its efficiency, is produced by and out of specks of granular slime arranging themselves as of their own accord in sheets and layers, and acting seemingly on an agreed plan. That done, and their organ complete, they abide by what they have accomplished. They lapse into relative quietude and change no more. It all sounds an unskilful overstated tale which challenges belief. But to faithful observation so it is.

Demonstration

At a first glance, seeing such technical words such as 'spheroid', 'biconvex', 'blood-vessels', 'light sensitive', we might be inclined to say that this is a typical piece of scientific writing on the structure of the human eye. The writer, we observe, makes considerable use of a comparison, or analogy, between the human eye and the camera; and in the course of his exposition he covers such items as lens, retina, iris, tears, eyelids and focussing. Essentially, we might say, this is a piece of prose taken from a textbook of physiology written for sixth form biologists or medical students: it is concerned with facts and nothing but facts; its intention is to do no more than to convey impersonally certain scientific, carefully-observed data.

To go no further than that, however, would be to overlook many interesting uses of language and significant details. We may soon notice that, although the topic of the passage is one we readily associate with 'science', there is, in fact, a considerable *absence* of technical language in the passage, and the writer at most seems to be trying to explain his subject without the use of technicalities. For another thing, the language, if we look carefully, does not have the cold impersonality of orthodox scientific prose. Many of the sentences are very short, and deliberately simple: though we could not possibly suppose that there was an undeveloped mind behind them. There is a simple informality about the flow of language which can even accommodate utterances which are not grammatical entities, such as – 'A spheroid camera.' And the repetition of 'Will traverse.' The writer seems to be speaking to us without much formality: filling in his word picture carefully, detail by detail, as he expounds it, being careful not to overload his readers with too much all at once. It would be easy to suppose, in fact, that this passage is transcribed from a lecture, or demonstration – and such indeed is the case.

A final thing which differentiates this passage from pure scientific prose is that, besides conveying a certain number of facts and thoughts, the writer also conveys an unmistakable and personal feeling about his subject. The second sentence already introduces the term 'perfection' – which is essentially a subjective term – and we soon see that an important part of the writer's intention is to convey his admiration and wonder at the facts he is presenting. The eye to him, though as we suppose a professional scientist, is not just an assemblage of phenomena, but something of a miracle of 'craftsmanship'. It displays two chief aspects of the miraculous: firstly, the delicate precision of the eye as an instrument of vision; and, secondly, the unerring but marvellous way in which the eye develops even before its owner has been born.

It is interesting to notice how the writer's thought seems to *grow*, almost imitating the process of growth he is telling us about. The passage opens with a few simple, bare statements, comparing the eye to a spheroid camera, and commenting on the importance of its exact shape. The 'light which will enter the eye will traverse a lens placed in the right position there'. The writer has allowed himself to drop into the future tense, and by appearing to be rather surprised at this – 'will traverse ...' brings our minds quickly to the problem of the future growth and development. The preparing of the eye for seeing in the light all takes place in the dark of the womb. Nobody directs the process, although what occurs can only be compared to the work of the most skilful craftsman. It is as if the eye, in response to some power of creation within itself, knows what has to be done, and just systematically sets about doing it; it specializes its cells, some to produce the glass-clear lens, others the adjustable iris which controls the width of the beam of light entering the eye, others the light-sensitive cells of the retina. The word 'slung' ('delicately slung with accurate centring') is a metaphor from engineering, and briefly calls up a picture of a group of workmen taking infinite pain to manoeuvre a certain piece of equipment into position for the construction of a building or factory. The paragraph ends with two neatly balanced parallel sentences:

> In microscope, or photographic camera,
> the adjustment is made by the observer ...
>
> In the eye this adjustment is automatic, worked by the image itself!

There is no clumsy attempt to bring out the startling nature of the contrast. A mere exclamation mark after 'the image itself!' serves to call our attention to the fact that something remarkable has just been said, and invites us to think it out for ourselves.

Now, as the second paragraph continues, the idea of the eye controlling its own growth is given by the indicative mood of the verbs:
> The lens and screen cut the chamber of the eye into a front half and a back half, both filled with clear humour ...

(we have come to the only really specialized word in the passage: *humour*, here in its medical sense of 'a bodily fluid'), but this is redeemed for the non-specialist by the homely vocabulary of the rest of the sentence

> *practically* water, kept under a *certain* pressure maintaining the eye-ball's *right* shape.

The statement that the front of the eye-ball is completed by what is nothing other than a layer of specialized skin, in which no blood vessels are found and which has only one of the normal skin-senses (i.e. of touch, or pain), reminds us how marvellously the whole structure has evolved from the most basic kind of cells, indeed almost from nothing.

Next the writer describes what we normally call, and take for granted as, 'eye-lids', but it is significant that he does not use this familiar name, but, in order to make us think more precisely about this amazing piece of equipment, he describes them very prosaically as

> movable flaps, dry outside like ordinary skin, but moist inside so as to wipe the windows clean every minute or so ...

'Windows', of course, introduces another metaphor alongside that of the camera: the eye obviously invites comparison with a window, through which we look out from inside upon the world outside.

We also notice that the writer avoids the word 'tears' – a word which naturally has many strong emotional implications:

> Thoughts that do often be too deep for tears
>
> Wordsworth
>
> Tears, idle tears, I know not what they mean
> Born from the depth of some divine despair ...
>
> Tennyson

Instead he brings in the unemotive, more precise term 'tear-water', which prevents us being drawn away into irrelevant memories, and makes us realize that 'tear-water' is a matter-of-fact substance in the eye, not only at moments of special emotion, but all the time and for a necessary purpose.

The analogy between the eye and the camera is further exposed in the third paragraph, though certain variations occur. 'Key-structure' is obviously an architectural metaphor – 'the key-stone' in an arch, for example, is the one essential to keep the whole structure stable. In fact the eye is more like a cinematographic camera: it 'receives, takes and records a *moving* picture', not of course for a few hours only, but, in another homely phrase, – 'life-long'. Now comes another easily grasped metaphor from the science of human communications: the retina 'signals' its 'exposures' (photography) to the brain.

In paragraph four, the self-adjusting aspect of the eye is given more attention, 'it focuses itself': it makes its lenses 'stronger' or 'weaker' as required. The use of inverted commas for 'stronger' and 'weaker' is of special interest: the writer is indicating that in fact there are much greater subtleties to the process than these simple words convey, but he is using such homely expressions as non-scientific people use when referring to the lenses of their spectacles ('I think I need some stronger glasses.')

The next detail, referring to the self-preserving 'fore-thought' of the eye, is more carefully qualified: it is, he writes, contrived as though with *fore-thought* of self-preservation. Perhaps we should beware of seeing too much conscious self-control in the operation of the eye, and in fact the next operation – blinking ('in a moment its *skin shutters* close, protecting its transparent window' – note again the deflationary language) is one of the most common examples we have of a reflex or completely unconscious action. Yet we soon switch back to the personification of the eye: if danger threatens, 'in a moment its skin shutters close'.

Now, in the middle of the fourth paragraph, the writer pulls himself out of particularization, and proceeds to some general thoughts. But again the continuation of his simple direct language, with the avoidance of the over-familiar, helps us to grasp the miracle of the eye quite vividly. 'The whole structure ... is produced by and out of specks of granular slime.' Human life is marvellous not because it has been achieved so easily as some accounts seem to suggest (e.g. 'God said Let there be Light, and there was light'), but because everything that exists has evolved gradually out of something more primitive – which of course is the best interpretation of the story of Creation, as we read it in the Bible. 'Slime' (compare its use on page 143) is a word with extremely unpleasant associations – for example, a person who falls into a pond full of mud and water weeds is likely to come up covered with filthy 'slime'. Another rather relevant use of the word is found in the familiar expression 'primeval slime' – often thought to be the basic substance out of which life evolved long ago on the shores of some prehistoric lagoon. What a stark contrast we are given, between the granular 'slime' and the marvellous brilliance and perception of the human eye as we now have it.

Next we come to another aspect of the phenomenon of the eye. For a time the specks of granular slime continue to arrange themselves in sheets and layers, 'acting seemingly on an agreed plan' – there may be some metaphorical allusions here to the instinctive organization of bees and ants as they build up their hives and nests. But once the work of creation is over, and their 'organ' is complete, the great activity ceases. 'They abide by what they have accomplished, and ... change no more.' What has suddenly happened to the language here? It is impossible not to recognize the archaic, and in fact, scriptural tone. The language is still simple, but it is the simplicity not of modern colloquial speech, but of the Bible ... 'abide ... change no more'. The biblical flavour is not accidental; it conveys a quick allusion to the Creator being satisfied with all he has done, and 'resting' on the seventh day. Is this too far-fetched a suggestion? I think not: the human mind has extraordinary powers of summoning up from its past memories just those words which are apt in a special set of circumstances.

At the end, the generalizing, self-critical mind of the writer again takes control for a while as he realizes that what he has said may sound like an 'unskilful, overstated tale which challenges belief': the scientific investigator appears afraid that the 'truth' he is revealing will seem to his readers 'stranger than fiction'. Yet, no sooner has he stated this objection than he immediately counters it with the utterly simple affirmation, based on his confidence in his scientific method,

      But to faithful observation so it is.

This examination will have reminded us how impossible it is to separate the methods of prose and poetry. Here, in a preponderantly scientific exposition we see that many of the resources of the poet (personification, metaphor, allusion, selection of vocabulary, control of the sentence rhythm) have all played, though, no doubt, quite unconsciously, an important part. The man of science and the poet are by no means at opposite poles.

12 Foruwa

Shall we say
Shall we put it this way
Shall we say that the maid of Kyerefaso, Foruwa, daughter of the Queen Mother, was a young deer, graceful in limb? Such was she, with head held high, eyes soft and wide with wonder. And she was light of foot, light in all her moving.

Stepping springily along the water path like a deer that had strayed from the thicket, springily stepping along the water path, she was a picture to give the eye a feast. And nobody passed her by but turned to look at her again.

Those of her village said that her voice in speech was like the murmur of a river quietly flowing beneath shadows of bamboo leaves. They said her smile would sometimes blossom like a lily on her lips and sometimes rise like sunrise.

The butterflies do not fly away from the flowers, they draw near. Foruwa was the flower of her village.

So shall we say,
Shall we put it this way, that all the village butterflies, the men, tried to draw near her at every turn, crossed and crossed her path? Men said of her, 'She shall be my wife, and mine, and mine and mine.'

But suns rose and set, moons silvered and died and as the days passed Foruwa grew more lovesome, yet she became no one's wife. She smiled at the butterflies and waved her hand lightly to greet them as she went swiftly about her daily work:

'Morning, Kweku
Morning, Kwesi
Morning, Kodwo'

but that was all.

And so they said, even while their hearts thumped for her:
'Proud!
Foruwa is proud ... and very strange.'

And so the men when they gathered would say:
'There goes a strange girl. She is not just stiff-in-the-neck

proud, not just breasts-stuck-out-I-am-the-only-girl-in-the-village proud. What kind of pride is hers?'

The end of the year came round again, bringing the season of festivals. For the gathering-in of corn, yams and cocoa there were harvest celebrations. There were bride-meetings too. And it came to the time when the Asafo companies should hold their festival. The village was full of manly sounds, loud musketry and swelling choruses.

Demonstration

The object of this passage is to give us an impression of Foruwa, the maid of Kyerefaso, who is obviously an unusual and attractive girl, and the relationship between her and the other people of her community. While their attitude of admiration is clearly a very normal one, she in some way seems to be peculiarly different. Although quite cheerful and friendly, she remains aloof and appears to be waiting for someone or something, which is not to be found in the local environment.

There is little that is obscure or puzzling in this passage, but much can be pointed to as contributing to the special feeling of delight with which we read it. The thing which strikes our attention most clearly is the unusual vivacity and lightness which has been infused into what clearly looks like a passage of prose. The general mood of the passage, as conveyed to us by various aspects of the language, is of the greatest dramatic relevance in giving us an impression of the beauty and liveliness of Foruwa herself.

We shall look first of all at the structure and organization of the sentences. From the very opening, the multiple question:

> Shall we say
> Shall we put it this way
> Shall we say that the maid of Kyerefaso, Foruwa ...?

we receive a hint that this is a kind of prose which is liable at any minute to take off into the realms of poetry: the three-fold rhetorical question, with its 'say-way-say' rhyme, suggests both the searching, experimental nature of the thought behind the writing, and the strong feeling for rhythm that the writer possesses.

The use of the plural pronoun ('we') is incidentally of significance, suggesting the close identity which the writer reckons to achieve with the readers. It is not an 'I *and* you' relationship, 'listen-to-me-dear-readers!', but a feeling of community and shared interests, typical of most African societies.

Even before we have reached the end of the first sentence, we notice the specially balanced arrangement of the parts of the sentence. In a strictly prosaic prose, we should have:

> (she) was graceful in limb as a young deer

How much more elegant and emphatic is the version we are given:
> (she) was as a young deer, graceful in limb

in which we can distinctly detect the leaping rhythm of the springing deer. The sentence following brings in alliterations to support the rhythmic effect:
> *S*uch was *s*he, with *h*eld *h*igh, eyes *s*oft and *w*ide with *w*onder

Then comes the first of many effective uses of word repetition:
> And she was *light* of foot, *light* in all her moving.

This effect is further developed at the beginning of the next paragraph by the repetition in inverted order of the participle and adverb:
> Stepping springily along the water path ...
> springily stepping along the water path ...

And a further delightful rhythmic pattern is set up later on, referring not to the movements of Foruwa, but to the passage of time during which she remains heart-free:
> But suns rose and set,
> moons silvered and died ...

which seems to add greatly to the idyllic quality of the whole passage.

We should notice that all these rhythmic effects are gained by the use of a language which is essentially very simple. The vocabulary is not in the least ostentatious, and the whole has something of the directness of a folk tale. Possibly there is also present something of the classic simplicity of scriptural language; if, for example, we ask why the writer uses 'her moving' instead of 'her movements' in the first paragraph; and if, again, we look at the rather unusual structure of the sentence
> nobody passed her but turned to look ...

we may recognize echoes of the idiom of the Bible, so much of which depends on its essential simplicity for the power of its effects.

Into the simple, springy narrative, the small, typical colloquial remarks which the story requires fit with the greatest of ease:
> 'Morning, Kweku
> Morning, Kwesi ...',

though the earlier comment made by the 'men' has an interesting compressed effect based on the repetition of the possessive pronoun:

> 'She shall be my wife, and mine, and mine and mine.'

The writer shows excellent understanding of the intonations of spoken English, as shown by the dramatically significant pause indicated in the phrase:

> 'Proud!
> Foruwa is proud ... and very strange.'

The three dots indicating the pause after 'proud' suggests the dawning of puzzlement in the minds of the village people as they realize that Foruwa is proud, but not proud in quite the same way as other village girls might be. Then in the following paragraph, we have a quick impression of the way that folk speech can blossom into a shrewd, caricaturing saltiness as they admit

> 'She is not just stiff-in-the-neck proud, nor just breasts-stuck-out-I-am-the-only-girl-in-the-village proud.'

This gives us a very incisive indication that Foruwa is not just the usual type of haughty beauty, very conscious of her physical charms, who knows how to use them in order to tantalize and humiliate her admirers. Her genial greetings to the village men sound perfectly easy and good-natured, and she 'waved her hand lightly to greet them'. Clearly she possesses some unusual qualities, though their full nature has not yet been disclosed.

Along with this natural idiom of speech goes the simple observation of facts, which gives an element of universality to the particular scene:

> ... their hearts thumped for her
> The end of the year came round again ...

and as we come to the end of the present extract, the simple sociological facts are neatly and simply sketched in ('there were bride-meetings too') until we reach a climax with

> The village was full of manly sounds, loud
> musketry, and swelling choruses

– a climax, which of course immediately sets our minds wondering what developments will follow at the end-of-year ceremonies.

In complete harmony with the rhythmic, colloquial simplicity of the passage is the strong element of simile and metaphor which runs through it – again it reminds us strongly of folk literature, with at the same time certain biblical echoes. It is Foruwa herself who provokes most of these. She is said to be:

> like a deer that has strayed from the thicket.

Her voice, we are told, was:

> like the murmur of a river quietly flowing beneath shadows of bamboo leaves

— a cool, refreshing and inviting scene.

Her smile, that most glorious and heart-warming of all human attributes, would sometimes

> 'blossom
> like a lily on her lips' —

and we could spend some time appreciating the appropriateness of this simile with its suggestions of colour, shape, purity and virginity. At other times her smile would come more slowly and more mysteriously, but no less beautifully, when it would:

> rise like sunrise.

The growth of simile into metaphor is well illustrated when the writer fuses this series of similes into one final, conclusive metaphor:

> Foruwa was the flower of her village.

The men of the village, in complement to her flower-like qualities become, of course, 'butterflies', and the proverb-like under-statement:

> The butterflies do not fly away from the flowers, they draw near

admirably expresses something of the helpless, inevitable attraction by which they are drawn towards the flower. The simile is also happy because usually when attractive flowers are in season, butterflies come flitting about in considerable number, and their eager but erratic flight well represents the confused feelings of Foruwa's baffled admirers.

The effect of this charmingly effective piece of writing need not be laboured. It has the qualities of clarity and freshness found, as we have already observed, in the best folk-literature; but at the same time, the sensitive organization of the expression indicates the artistry of an individual writer of considerable sophistication, with great feeling for the English language.

Further evidence of this sophistication may be illustrated in the parallel which exists between the opening lines of this passage, and the opening lines of one of the most famous poems of the century: *The Love Song of J. Alfred Prufrock*, by T. S. Eliot. An interesting series of further speculations might be opened up on the ironic effects which our present writer gains from this allusion. Prufrock, like Foruwa, is inclined to withdraw from intimate contact with the other people of his community; but whereas he is presented as one of the baffled and enfeebled figures of an almost exhausted culture, Foruwa has the freshness and vigour of the heroine of a fertility myth, produced by a culture which is full of 'new life'.

13 'Utopia'[1]

I enjoyed perfect health of body, and tranquillity of mind; I did not feel the treachery or inconstancy of a friend, nor the injuries of a secret or open enemy. I had no occasion of bribing, flattering or pimping, to procure the favour of any great man, or of his minion. I wanted no fence against fraud or oppression; here was neither physician to destroy my body, nor lawyer to ruin my fortune: no informer to watch my words and actions, or forge accusations against me for hire: here were no gibers, censurers, backbiters, pickpockets, highwaymen, housebreakers, attorneys, bawds, buffoons, gamesters, politicians, wits, spleneticks, tedious talkers, controvertists, ravishers, murderers, robbers, virtuosos; no encouragers to vice, by seducement or examples: no dungeon, axes, gibbets, whipping-posts, or pillories: no cheating shopkeepers or mechanicks: no pride, vanity or affectation: no fops, bullies, drunkards, strolling whores, or poxes: no ranting, lewd, expensive wives: no stupid, proud pedants: no importunate, over-bearing, quarrelsome, noisy, roaring, empty, conceited, swearing companions: no scoundrels raised from the dust upon the merit of their vices; or nobility thrown into it, on account of their virtues: no lords, fiddlers, judges, or dancing-masters.

---

[1] this title is supplied by the editor.
NOTES: *pimping*   ministering to carnal desires.
          informer   spy; one who denounces.
          spleneticks   bad-tempered people.
          virtuosos   clever people, often monomaniacs.
          gibbets, pillories   instruments of punishment associated with barbarous ages.
          lewd   immoral.

Demonstration

The notes, helping to overcome some vocabulary difficulties, remind us that this passage is not contemporary; indeed many advanced students using this book will quickly recognize its source. Nevertheless if we can approach it with detachment it is a fascinating piece to read, and even more to analyze.

Yes, this *is* a piece of prose. All the usual tests confirm this. Nor is it highly metaphorical, full of brilliant epithets, or in any usual sense a piece of poetic prose. Nevertheless it presents certain unusual features.

Let us proceed without panic! What is the situation? We cannot from the passage itself glean much information: the writer is obviously looking back on a time, or a place, as he tells us in the opening sentence, when he enjoyed ideal conditions:

perfect health of body, and tranquillity of mind.

No other positive information is given of the cricumstances which he 'enjoyed', and it very quickly passes into the negative, as the writer proceeds to tell us at length and in detail what he did *not* have to put up with in this later, ideal state. Then, once having launched into a catalogue of the things he *no longer* had to experience, he seems hardly to be able to stop himself, for an amazingly long list of grievances comes pouring forth. It soon becomes clear that the writer is not directly concerned to call up in any detail the circumstances or atmosphere of the peaceful existence he enjoyed, except in negative terms. In fact what he is really doing – and this seems to be his chief intention, is to give a detailed denunciation of the state of affairs that he had to endure before he found his present peaceful one. It is not difficult to guess that his ideal existence is one which is secluded from the main stream of human life, and that the state of existence he is glad to be free from is the cosmopolitan world of fashionable city life.

The long catalogue of types we are told of consists of the kinds of people, so frequently met with in large communities, who make 'health' and 'tranquillity' impossible. The passage, therefore, consists of a denunciation of all the wicked and immoral people who are found in human society. The passage, that is to say, is clearly satirical in intention.

It may now occur to us to ask how seriously the passage should be taken. Do we accept it in the spirit it is offered, as a piece of savage, bitter, heart-broken anger directed at almost the whole human race? Or, is there perhaps an element of playful humour about it, as though the writer is chiefly concerned to make us laugh with him at a kind of elaborate joke? Is the writer so carried away by his own eloquence, his own skilful technique, that he does not care too much to think what he is saying? For example, the passage makes no mention of any virtues, except perhaps by implication in the writer himself. Is the passage therefore heavily unbalanced in its selection of detail? This is a matter of delicate judgement, and we can best consider it after surveying the passage in more detail.

Let us first see how the passage is organized. We have already used the term 'catalogue' to indicate our first reaction to it. How useful is this term? 'Catalogue' signifies a comprehensive list of items, usually of a very utilitarian nature, probably quite boring to anyone who has no need of the special information it contains, and organized only on a most mechanical principle. Many students will remember having been warned against the kind of catalogue story or essay which is linked together very aimlessly in some such way as '... then ... and then ... and then ...'. At first sight we may imagine we see something of this element in the uniformity of the sentence openings, all beginning with the first person pronoun.

> I enjoyed perfect health ...
> I did not feel the treachery ...
> I had no occasion of bribing ...
> I wanted no fence ...

However, if we have read even this far with an ear attentive to the rhythm of the sentence structures, we shall discover that the repetition of the same sentence pattern comes not from slackness, or laziness of expression, but from the desire for emphatic statement. As each sentence follows the other, it seems to come with an accumulating energy, leading towards an overwhelming climax. In fact, we begin to notice that this prose is highly and elaborately organized in many ways: it is no flabby catalogue, but a careful balancing of word, phrase, and clause, often with a strong effect of antithesis, which indicates to us the presence of a powerful, deliberating mind at work.

This is apparent from the very beginning:

> I enjoyed ... health of body ... tranquillity of mind
>
> I did not feel ... treachery of a friend ... injury of an enemy

Within this general pattern, there are several subsidiary antitheses:

> ... the treachery or inconsistency of a friend ...
>
> ... the injuries of a secret or open enemy ...

We next notice that in the third sentence, though only after a semicolon, the sentence pattern changes from the first person opening to the impersonal:

> here was neither physician ... nor lawyer

and the pattern is repeated a few lines later

> here were no gibers, censurers, backbiters ...

and in fact, in spite of the many colons, this is the beginning of the sentence that continues right through to the end of the paragraph. Rather an amazing sentence, with a highly intricate, multiple subject; the simple little verb 'were', and a single adverb 'here'.

The organizing, or patterning, word is henceforth 'no', used with increasing emphasis as the writer works through his list of mischief-makers. Again within this general pattern there is a certain amount of subsidiary variations, especially in the length of each separate group; and in the alternation between the specific wrongdoer, and the more general vice:

> no cheating shopkeepers or mechanicks:
>
> no pride, vanity or affectation:
>
> no fops, bullies, drunkards, strolling whores, or poxes:
>
> no ranting, lewd, expensive wives:
>
> no stupid, proud pedants:
>
> no importunate, over-bearing, quarrelsome, noisy, roaring, empty, conceited, swearing companions:

An additional effect of exasperation is gained at some points by the unusual length of a stream of nouns such as

> no gibers, censurers, backbiters, pickpockets, highwaymen, house-breakers, attorneys, bawds, buffoons, gamesters, politicians, wits, spleneticks, tedious talkers, controvertists, ravishers, murderers, robbers, virtuosos:

And, towards the end, a different kind of variation is produced when two contrasted nouns are each qualified by a concise participial phrase:

> no scoundrels raised from the dust upon the merit of their vices
>
> or nobility thrown into it, on account of their virtues

(The metaphor of being raised from the dust, incidentally, is not highly original but on the other hand it is not greatly emphasized, and seems to fit neatly into position.)

This examination in detail demonstrates something of the highly organized rhythmic form of the passage. Its effect is to give great energy and emphasis to the expression of the writer's thoughts, and, even more, to his feelings. If we are inclined to sympathize with the writer's views even to a limited extent, we may be inclined to envy his great powers of sentence organization. We might almost be disposed to memorize the passage, with the idea of gaining a great deal of pleasure and satisfaction in declaiming it – far more than from the utterance of some of the customary, drab swear words!

Now, from the sentence structure we turn to look more closely at some interesting vocabulary effects. While the writer's vocabulary seems to be extensive, it is used in an economical way; for example, there is little use of adjectives to qualify nouns (except in the long string which qualifies 'companions'). But in deciding upon his careful juxtaposition of words, the writer obtains unusual effects quite early in the passage: perhaps we are already used to the idea of the lawyer whose principal aim is to impoverish ('ruin') his client, but just before that we are told of the efforts of the 'physician'

> to destroy my body.

Normally, of course, we associate the physician with the healing of the body, but this sudden paradoxical effect reminds us that in an imperfect world the physician may be ignorant, incompetent, lazy, greedy, malicious, and fail to live up to the ideals of his profession.

We should also notice how, in the lengthy lists of obvious rogues, the writer slips in quietly the names of some people whom we should normally regard as respectable:

> ... highwaymen, house-breakers, *attorneys*, bawds, buffoons, gamesters, politicians, *wits*, spleneticks, tedious talkers ...

This exasperated juxtaposition has the effect of making us think twice; to go beneath our accepted ideas and stock notions, and to sharpen our thoughts – after all, many apparently law-abiding people may have just as unpleasant characteristics as the more recognizable type of criminals. The same mischievous spirit is seen in the presence among a later list of malefactors of

> ranting, lewd, *expensive* wives,

and later still:

> lords, fiddlers, judges, or dancing-masters.

How scathing to group together such widely differing people, and to speak of 'lords' and 'judges' in the same breath with 'fiddlers' and 'dancing-masters'.

One particularly interesting word-use occurs with the word 'companions' which is made to take on a new set of connotations. Usually 'companions' suggests friendship, love, common interests, mutual help – in general a harmonious relationship. Here, the long string of unfavourable epithets (which we have already quoted) has the effect of devaluing the word, and perhaps is evidence of the author's misanthropy – as though all he wishes is to get away from human society altogether, to enjoy his tranquillity in isolation.

This brings us back to the difficult question of judgement. How seriously can we take this passage? Is it so violent, so extreme, so unbalanced that we dismiss it as a clever joke in bad taste, lacking realism and sincerity? Or is it a piece of acceptable satirical moralizing?

If we have any doubts about this, there are several points to give further attention to. Firstly, we notice that although the passage is vigorously abusive, no particular person is mentioned in it: even if the writer has exaggerated, no individual person has suffered, except possibly the writer himself! If the passage tends towards misanthropy, it is certainly not malevolent.

Secondly, there are some important touch-stones which we have not yet commented on. In the bad world, we are told, scoundrels are often raised from the dust

> upon the merit of their vices.

This is a challenging paradox: how can the 'merit' of scoundrels be in their 'vices'? Their vices, we answer, bring them the kind of respect and honour which ought to be given to men of obvious

'merit'. In the following word group, the theme is continued: 'nobility' are often thrown 'into the dust', into disgrace –
> on account of their virtues.

Both words, 'merit' and 'virtues', are here used without any trace of irony or mockery, and this definite, even if passing, recognition of the possibility of genuine 'virtue' does preserve an element of balance in the passage as a whole.

We therefore conclude that it is a piece of highly polished and effective satire, redeemed from the shallowness that such kinds of writing often suffer from.

14 The Cathedral

When he saw the cathedral in the distance, dark blue lifted watchful in the sky, his heart leapt. It was the sign in heaven, it was the Spirit hovering like a dove, like an eagle over the earth. He turned his glowing ecstatic face to her, his mouth opened with a strange, ecstatic grin.

'There she is', he said.

The 'she' irritated her. Why 'she'? It was 'it'. What was the cathedral, a big building, a thing of the past, obsolete, to excite him to such a pitch? She began to stir herself to readiness.

They passed up the steep hill, he eager as a pilgrim arriving at the shrine. As they came near the precincts, with castle on one side and cathedral on the other, his veins seemed to break into a fiery blossom, he was transported.

They had passed through the gate, and the great west front was before them, with all its breadth and ornament.

'It is a false front', he said, looking at the golden stone and the twin towers, and loving them just the same. In a little ecstasy he found himself in the porch, on the brink of the unrevealed. He looked up to the lovely unfolding of the stone. He was to pass within to the perfect womb.

Then he pushed open the door, and the great pillared gloom was before him, in which his soul shuddered and rose from her nest. His soul leapt, soared up into the great church. His body stood still, absorbed by the height. His soul leapt up into the gloom, into possession, it reeled, it swooned with a great escape, it quivered in the womb, in the hush and the gloom of fecundity, like seed of procreation in ecstasy.

She too was overcome with wonder and awe. She followed him in his progress. Here, the twilight was the very essence of life, the coloured darkness was the embryo of all light, and the day. Here, the very first dawn was breaking, the very last sunset sinking, and the immemorial darkness, whereof life's day would blossom and fall away again, re-echoed peace and profound immemorial silence.

Away from time, always outside of time! Between east and west, between dawn and sunset, the church lay like a seed in silence, dark before germination, silenced after death. Containing birth and death, potential with all the noise and transition of life, the cathedral remained hushed, a great involved seed, whereof the flower would be radiant life inconceivable, but whose beginning and whose end were the circle of silence. Spanned round with the rainbow, the jewelled gloom folded music upon silence, light upon darkness, fecundity upon death, as a seed folds leaf upon leaf and silence upon the root and the flower, hushing up the secret of all between its parts, the death out of which it fell, the life into which it has dropped, the immortality it involves, and the death it will embrace again.

Demonstration

Here we are shown a man and a woman approaching a cathedral – we cannot tell which one. We understand that they are enthusiastic about their visit, though there is some difference between the attitude of the man and the woman. At length they reach it, their expectation mounting higher and higher. After a short pause, they open the door at the 'west front' and enter, and the passage goes on to convey to us the feelings and sensations which the author imagines his characters to experience, as they stand inside, overcome with awe. This is the factual basis of the situation. The writer's main aim is not so much to outline the facts, nor even to attempt very much description of the building, but to convey to us, as completely as he can, the state of mind of the two visitors. They are clearly no casual tourists – sight-seers, antiquarians, photographers, but people with a highly developed spiritual and philosophical imagination. This is obviously a task for which considerable resources of language are needed, and possibly we shall be interested to observe the efforts which the author has made to be equal to the occasion.

With the barest economy of language, the passage presents a clear factual account of the basic narrative details, which could not be simpler:

> He saw the cathedral in the distance ...
>
> They passed up the steep hill ...
>
> They had passed through the gate ...
>
> Then he pushed open the door ...
>
> She followed him in his progress ...

But upon this plain, basic fabric, the writer has woven some notable variations. At points we observe the presence of a number of brief comments which seem to come from a very simple, internal monologue:

> The 'she' irritated her. Why 'she'? It was 'it'.

and

> Away from time, always outside of time!

Much more conspicuous, however, is the development of the prose, from being a vehicle of factual information, into a highly rhythmic and poetic medium of expression, while it continues to accommodate both the factual elements of description and the suggestions of internal monologue. It is the writer's command of the rhythm which, first and last, impresses us most. The effects are gained in a number of different ways. Firstly we notice the placing of words in positions of special emphasis, contrary to the customary prose order. For example, in the sentence

> ... he saw the cathedral in the distance, dark blue lifted watchful in the sky ...

'dark blue' an epithet of colour, would prosaically precede the noun 'cathedral': but placed here at the beginning of a sentence of qualifying expressions it acquires a marked rhythmic juxtaposition with its head-word. At other times the rhythmic effect is gained by the rapid accumulation of verbs, without the use of the formal link-words associated with more pedestrian prose. We have noticed this already with 'lifted watchful'; and it appears again in such instances as:

> his soul *leaped, soared* up into the great church

and again

> his soul leaped up ..., it reeled, it swooned with a great escape, it quivered ...

– a sentence which, taken as a whole, conveys a magnificent moving picture of the expansion and frenzy of the man's feelings as he first steps through the door. The quick repetition of verbs and the unequal length of the sentences seems to suggest the movements of a bird which has been let loose inside a great space, and seeks frantically to discover the limits of its confines. Some other non-rhythmical effects also enter into the effect of this sentence, as we shall see later.

The writer displays considerable sensitivity and 'happiness' in his selection of vocabulary, both in the meaning and the sounds of the words he uses. How neatly, for example, is the difference of attitude between the man and the woman indicated by their choice of pronoun: where as the man refers to the cathedral with admiration and devotion as 'she', the woman thinks to herself that it is after all only an 'it' – a world of difference! Then although, as we have said, the passage is not primarily concerned with description, we cannot fail to notice the admirable effect of the words in the sentence

> They had passed through the gate, and the great west front was before them, with all its breadth and ornament.

– which incidentally is given force by constituting a complete paragraph by itself. Let us notice also the use of the past perfect tense ('they had passed') where most of the other verbs are in the usual narrative past tense: this has the effect of speeding up the narrative, as though the visitors are now hastening forward eagerly, and have actually passed through the gates into the precincts before there has even been a chance to mention it. Next comes the grand monosyllabic simplicity of

> The great west front was before them,

which suggests the elemental grandeur of the building which exists massively in its own right. The visitors did not 'see', or 'catch sight of' or 'have their first glimpse of' the cathedral: *it was before them* – with an effect of stupendous suddenness. The same sparse simplicity is used in indicating some of its qualities:

> with all its breadth and ornament.

The man commented simply that, as with many cathedrals, the west front was structurally unrelated to the main building behind it, but 'he loved it just the same', and his loving appreciation is well indicated by the quick, passing verbal caress, with its assonance and alliteration,

> 'It is a false front,' he said, looking at
> the golden stone and the twin towers.

Even the strictly needless repetition of 'the' here adds something to the balance of the phrase, which is in harmony of the symmetry of the cathedral's facade.

Far more than the selection of individual words, however, the most conspicuous feature of the passage's success is its rich and deliberate use of metaphor and simile. The experience which the writer has to convey cannot be embodied only in literal language, and we can sense how this urgent need for adequate means of expression draws him at almost every point into vigorous, figurative language. At the first sight of the cathedral, for example, 'his heart leapt'. His face was 'glowing'. The woman in her incipient reaction against the man's feelings 'began to stir herself'. As they climbed the hill, he is 'eager as a pilgrim'; within the precincts, 'his veins seemed to break into blossoms', – not only 'blossoms' but '*fiery* blossoms' – in cool terms this would be recognized as a mixed metaphor, but, as the equivalent of his expanding feelings, it seems easily acceptable in this context. As the man looks up at the masses and waves of intricate and patterned stone carving, he is aware, we read, of the 'lovely unfolding' of the stone – a transfer of the 'blossoming flower' metaphor from the man's spirit to the building he is observing. Once inside the cathedral his soul, we are told, 'rose from her nest': the metaphor is of a bird rising up and soaring to vast heights: students of literature may be able to identify the bird more precisely as the skylark celebrated often in literature and folklore for its joyful and arduous aspirations.

As the writer warms to his task, his grasp and enthusiasm leads to a manner of presentation which involves more than incidental metaphor. In the two final paragraphs we find some highly imaginative writing in which both metaphor and allusion are gradually evolved into symbolism. The woman, we are told, in spite of her earlier scepticism, begins to think of the interior of the cathedral, and its mysterious twilight, as representative of 'the very essence of life': the word 'essence' is used in no casual, hackneyed sense here. 'The coloured darkness was the embryo of all light.' In it, by a great paradox, 'the very first dawn was breaking' ('Let there be Light'), and at the same time 'the very last sunset was sinking'. The allusion here to the biblical Creation story is unmistakable.

The writer does not quickly pass on from this idea, however, but proceeds to develop it as fully and explicitly as possible. Containing as it were, 'the essence of life', the Cathedral, we are told, is independent, away from, always outside of 'time'! Remembering the seeds that can be dormant for thousands of years and yet spring up rapidly when circumstances are favourable, the author compares the whole Cathedral in a highly rhythmic and beautifully balanced sentence, to a seed:

> Between east and west, between dawn and sunset, the church lay like a seed in silence, dark before germination, silenced after death.

He proceeds to elaborate this metaphor: in the following sentence the cathedral is apprehended as a great involved seed

and we are reminded of the miraculous quality of that small particle of vegetable substance which contains within itself all the potentialities for the development of a complex system, bearing flowers and fruits which can 'unfold' from it. It is interesting to see how the word 'involved' has been recharged with meaning in this context: as we normally use it, it means 'complicated' in a rather humdrum way: here it has the sense of 'being intricately folded in upon itself'. The imaginative span required here to follow the author's metaphor, comparing the 'hushed silence' of the cathedral to the silent, dormant potentialities of the seed is considerable, but not, I think, too great for the average imaginative reader.

But the metaphorical use of 'seed' goes even further than this. We remember another use of the word 'seed' (as in such expression as 'the seed of Abraham') to refer to the elemental substance of procreation. In fact it has already been used in this sense earlier in the present passage, when the man's soul was compared to the 'seed of procreation in ecstasy' (we are reminded of the furious activity of the male sperm), and the cathedral itself to the womb. Thus the approach and entry of the visitors (especially the man) to the cathedral is thought of, in one of the boldest metaphors we have yet seen, as comparable to the act of procreation, the penetration of the male into the female. Thus the feeling of ecstasy experienced as they stand and release themselves into the vast space of the cathedral is analogous to the consummation of the act of physical love. Looking back to an earlier stage of the passage, we see how this is prepared for by the way in which the man instinctively referred to the cathedral, when they first caught sight of it, as 'she'.

If these interpretations of the symbolism seem strange or even irreverent, we should remember how often in the other literature the experiences of religious devotion and sexual passion have been used to describe each other, for example in the Bible, in the lyrics of the seventeenth century, or even in the words of an English bishop who thought it not blasphemous to describe the act of love as 'holy communion'.[1]

---

[1] At the trial *Regina v Penguin Books*, over the publication of D. H. Lawrence's novel *Lady Chatterley's Lover*.

We have not yet closely studied the final sentence of the final paragraph, where along with a further development of the 'great involved seed' symbol, we come upon what at first seems an unexpected reference to the rainbow. Perhaps the nature of colours from the stained-glass windows first suggests the rainbow, spanning or surrounding the cathedral. Then possibly the concentric bands of colour in the rainbow, all imperceptibly blending into each other, suggest the concentric 'folding', by the 'jewelled gloom', of music upon silence, light upon darkness, and so on. The rainbow becomes a symbol of the all-inclusive mystery which the visitors sense in the cathedral. In fact, the rainbow has already been alluded to earlier on in the passage, though our first few readings may not have been keen enough to recognize it. When the man first caught sight of the cathedral, we read, 'his heart leapt' at the sudden inspiring sight. Why did that sound so familiar? Perhaps we remember some words written by the poet Wordsworth a century and a half ago:

> My heart leaps up when I behold
> A rainbow in the sky.

The description of our passage goes on 'it was the sign in heaven, it was the Spirit hovering like a dove ...' and we now see that the comparison of the Cathedral takes us back, right beyond Wordsworth, to the great archetypal rainbow which God set in the heavens, after the great Flood, as a 'covenant' between himself and his creation. So, to our two visitors, the Cathedral, both in its distant prospect and in its interior atmosphere, shares in the symbolism of the rainbow. By this process of reference backwards and forwards in the passage, 'away from time', we begin to see how intricate is its organization.

We have not yet completely dealt with the final sentence of all, which to begin with may look complex and a little baffling. However, if we stick to our basic principle of working primarily from sentence structure – subject and predicate and so on, we shall discover that the sentence is basically simple: it merely tells us, with a kind of rich finality, how the 'jewelled gloom' of the cathedral seems to include in itself 'as a seed folds leaf upon leaf' all the elements, all the diversity and mystery of human life.

The two 'pilgrims', in other words, are experiencing exactly the thoughts and sensations which the original cathedral builders, and the men of vision who inspired them, intended us, ordinary men, to experience in the course of our spiritual enlightenment.

Our examination of this selected passage is not the end of the story by any means. Some students may be lucky enough to come upon it in their reading at a later stage in its full context, and discover how perfectly it fits into the complete structure of the novel from which it is taken – which, incidentally, is named after one of the symbols we have just been discussing.

15 The Beauty Industry

What are the practical results of the modern cult of beauty? The exercises and the massage, the health motors and the skin foods – to what have they led? Are women more beautiful than they were? Do they get something for the enormous expenditure of energy, time, and money demanded of them by the beauty-cult? These are questions which it is difficult to answer. For the facts seem to contradict themselves. The campaign for more physical beauty seems to be both a tremendous success and a lamentable failure. It depends how you look at the results.

It is a success in so far as more women retain their youthful appearance to a greater age than in the past. 'Old ladies' are already becoming rare. In a few years, we may well believe, they will be extinct. White hair and wrinkles, a bent back and hollow cheeks will come to be regarded as medievally old-fashioned. The crone of the future will be golden, curly and cherry-lipped, neat-ankled and slender. The Portrait of the Artist's Mother will come to be almost indistinguishable, at future picture shows, from the Portrait of the Artist's Daughter. This desirable consummation will be due in part to skin foods and injections of paraffin-wax, facial surgery, mud baths, and paint, in part to improved health, due in its turn to a more rational mode of life. Ugliness is one of the symptoms of disease, beauty of health. In so far as the campaign for more beauty is also a campaign for more health, it is admirable and, up to a point, genuinely successful. Beauty that is merely the artificial shadow of these symptoms of health is intrinsically of poorer quality than the genuine article. Still, it is a sufficiently good imitation to be sometimes mistakable for the real thing. The apparatus for mimicking the symptoms of health is now within the reach of every moderately prosperous person; the knowledge of the way in which real health can be achieved is growing, and will in time, no doubt, be universally acted upon. When that happy moment comes, will every woman be beautiful – as beautiful, at any rate, as the natural shape of her features, with or without surgical and chemical aid, permits?

The answer is emphatically: No. For real beauty is as much an affair of the inner as of the outer self. The beauty of a porcelain jar is a matter of shape, of colour, of surface texture. The jar may be empty or tenanted by spiders, full of honey or stinking slime – it makes no difference to its beauty or ugliness. But a woman is alive, and her beauty is therefore not skin deep. The surface of the human vessel is affected by the nature of its spiritual contents. I have seen women who, by the standards of a connoisseur of porcelain, were ravishingly lovely. Their shape, their colour, their surface texture were perfect. And yet they were not beautiful. For the lovely vase was either empty or filled with some corruption. Spiritual emptiness or ugliness shows through. And conversely, there is an interior light that can transfigure forms that the pure aesthetician would regard as imperfect or downright ugly.

Demonstration

Although this passage is taken from a longer piece of writing it contains all the evidence necessary for comprehension and appreciation within its own limits.

The opening sentence, without preamble, introduces us to a challenging question – 'What are the practical results of the modern cult of beauty?' As we read further through the opening paragraph, we see that the 'beauty' under discussion is clearly restricted to the 'beauty' of women, and, if we are for a moment puzzled by the word 'cult', we soon grasp its essence from the suggestion in a later sentence that it is something that demands 'energy, time and money'; towards the end of the paragraph it is also in a marked alliterative relationship with 'campaign', which serves almost as a synonym. By now, no reader, whatever culture he may come from, can have failed to see that the passage is dealing with what is sometimes called 'the Beauty Industry', that vast network of commercial interests which advertise and sell all over the world vast quantities of cosmetics and other physical aids to the improvement of physical beauty.

Now we have identified the topic, and even before the end of the first paragraph, we are given a hint of the kind of development to look for – the 'campaign has been both a tremendous success and a lamentable failure'. We are warned to expect a debating kind of discussion with 'pros and cons', or points For and Against. And so it turns out: the second paragraph proceeds to deal with the 'success' aspects of the beauty cult, and the third goes on to deal with its shortcomings or omissions.

The intention of the writer seems to be to concentrate our attention and to move our sympathies towards this latter aspect. Although he seems to be weighing up the situation formally and judiciously, we feel that paragraph two is merely disposing of those points as quickly as possible, and indeed we notice an undercurrent of irony ('the crone of the future ...') which suggests that the writer does not attach a great deal of importance to this section of the argument. After he has put the question which ushers in the third paragraph, the very decisive opening sentence of that paragraph –

The answer is emphatically: No
leaves us in no doubt that this is where his own convictions are strongest. In this paragraph, too, we shall see a number of other linguistic devices which persuade us that here he is expressing some strong moral feelings, and that ultimately he is very sceptical and scornful about the Beauty Industry and to some extent also those who subscribe to it.

If we have now read the passage over several times, we begin to form a general impression of the mind of its writer. We might describe it as lively, curious, inquisitive, exploratory; we see how readily he draws a wide range of allusion into his discussion of the subject. Although the passage presents the immediate appearance of prose, we shall see in how inventive and resourceful a manner the writer has organized his treatment of it, so that we feel that he has indeed communicated to us effectively both the general scope of the subject under discussion and his own personal feelings about it.

Let us now look further into the passage, and first at some aspects of its logical structure. It begins with a rhetorical question (an emphatic form of indirect statement): 'What are the practical results of the modern beauty cult?'. Soon we find that this general opening question is followed up by a series of parallel supplementary questions, each analyzing the matter a stage further:

> The exercises and the health motors ... to what have they led?
> Are women more beautiful than they were?
> Do they get something for the enormous expenditure ...?

Following the series of questions, we are told that there is no easy answer, for 'the facts seem to contradict themselves': the evidence is not all on one side, and the matter has to be weighed up. All this is intellectually quite satisfactory, and promises us a well-contested debate.

The second paragraph fulfils our expectations, as it follows up one side of the promised debate: 'It is a *success* in so far as ...' and we perceive that this paragraph will be dealing with one side of the question. So it proves: we learn how the signs of old age are becoming rare; '"Old ladies" are already becoming rare', and the idea is developed in four more parallel sentences, which give the writer some chance to display his sense of humour. At the sentence beginning 'This desirable consummation ...' we are linked back to the first paragraph by the reference to artificial beauty aids, but a new theme is also introduced: that the increase in physical beauty is a symptom of 'improved health, due in its turn to a more rational mode of life', and we see that here is a very justifiable development of the argument, since improved health is certainly a matter to be put to the credit of the beauty cult. After this, however, the current of thought seems to lose its onward movement as we are told that many people will often insist upon imitating the outward signs of health and beauty rather than cultivate them in the best way. The paragraph ends upon the thought of a time in the future when every woman can, in one way or another, acquire the characteristics of beauty, and the transition to paragraph three is introduced by the speculative question 'Will every woman be really beautiful?'.

Paragraph three opens abruptly, seeming to answer paragraph two directly 'The answer is emphatically: No.' We notice now that the plan of thought promised at the end of paragraph one ('tremendous success ... lamentable failure') has really been forgotten, for now we are launched upon a comparison of outward and inward beauty: this, of course, has some connection with the 'lamentable failure' of the beauty cult, but the relationship is not clearly marked out. Paragraph three, however, in itself is very self-consistent, and proceeds to develop its theme with great urgency and intellectual excitement: the interesting use of the word 'conversely', more usually associated with mathematical reasoning, indicates the active mental processes in the writer's mind.

Thus, as far as the logical structure of the whole passage is concerned, we may say that it is built up on a stream of rather vivid and exciting 'thinking', though without the strongly controlled development we would expect in more completely organized thought. This is not necessarily an adverse criticism of the passage – perhaps it contains other elements which amply atone for the slight wandering of thought.

Undoubtedly the passage makes a strong impact on any reader, who usually comes away feeling that he has been shown and taught something he had never so clearly realized before. We may observe a number of factors which contribute to this.

First, the general 'register' of the passage as expressed in the words and sentence construction used. The interesting thing to notice is that, although the subject of the passage is quite 'philosophical' and some of the sentences express quite abstract ideas, the language generally is very flexible and direct; we can almost hear the writer talking to us in the form mostly of simple questions and simple emphatic colloquial statements: *e.g.* 'the facts seem to contradict themselves ... Ugliness is one of the symptoms of disease ....Spiritual emptiness or ugliness shows through ...'

The author's flexibility of mind is also seen in the allusions he constantly draws in: some of them may tax our background knowledge quite severely. 'Old Ladies', in the author's own inverted commas, is a subtle allusion to members of the female sex who are old in years, certainly, but who also have other qualities of decay, such as timidity, fussiness, and mental decay. The 'crone' is an allusion to the bent and shrivelled witch-like old woman sometimes described in old historical stories and melodramas, and makes an ironical contrast with the 'old lady' of the future, who, perhaps like Miss Marlene Dietrich, will seem quite ageless. 'The Portrait of the Artist's Mother' is a direct allusion to a well-known painting of his aged mother by the late nineteenth-century painter Whistler, who clearly presents the physical wastage of the old lady, and this is humorously contrasted with 'The Portrait of the Artist's Daughter', which seems a kind of play on the title of the famous novel by James Joyce, *Portrait of the Artist as a Young Man*.

Another satirical aspect of the language is the author's trick of deliberately selecting flat, unglamorous words in which to refer to the 'beauty industry'. The 'desirable consummation' of perpetual youth will be achieved by such matter-of-fact processes as 'skin-foods, injections, *paraffin-wax*, facial surgery, *mud baths* and *paint*'; and later he mentions the beauty of a woman's features, 'with or without *surgical* or *chemical* help'. The effect of these words is already to suggest a certain disgust with the elaborate material apparatus of beauty culture, so much of which seems to contribute so little to its aim.

Undoubtedly, one of the most striking features of the passage is the powerful comparison, or analogy, between the beauty of a woman and the beauty of a porcelain jar, which is one of the most beautiful and delicate achievements of the art of pottery. The comparison is developed with a great deal of ingenuity and emotional force. A woman, like a porcelain jar, can be appreciated for such external features as 'shape, colour, and surface texture', and the comparison implies a humorous reference to the well-known way in which the male of the species is always interested in the shape of the female, while the 'texture', a quality investigated usually by the sense of touch, refers to the male desire to touch, or to caress the female. The rest of the comparison, however, leads us to contrast: we can appreciate the qualities of a porcelain jar without concerning ourselves with its contents, even if they are unpleasant; in the case of a woman, however, unless we are the most inhuman sensualists, we are bound to take into consideration her personal character and disposition before we give our whole-hearted admiration. The writer gives us to understand, if we didn't already know, that some women are, like porcelain jars, 'empty, or tenanted by spiders, full of ... stinking slime'.

We should, lastly, observe the extent to which the thought and the feeling of this passage are driven home by a stronger rhythmic organization. This organization seems to be based on the two factors of repeated series, and of exact antitheses. Paragraph one, as we have seen, contains a series of questions:

> What are the practical results ...?
> ... to what have they led?
> *Are* women more beautiful ...?
> *Do* they get something ...?

In the following paragraph this seems to be balanced by a corresponding series of four statements:

> 'Old ladies' are becoming rare ...
> White hair and wrinkles ... will come to be regarded as medievally old-fashioned.
> The crone of the future will be ...
> The Portrait of the Artist's Mother will come to be ...

Woven in and out of this rhythmic series, we observe how often the deliberative quality of the author's mind expresses itself in neatly balanced antitheses, *e.g.*

> The campaign ... seems to be both a tremendous success and a lamentable failure ...
> Ugliness is the symptom of disease, beauty of health.
> In so far as the campaign for more beauty is also a campaign for more health ...
> ... with or without surgical and chemical help ...
> ... as much an affair of the inner as the outer self ...
> ... either empty or filled with some corruption ...

In paragraph three there is another interesting rhythmic effect in the repetition, but in a different context (as we have already seen) of the expression
> shape, colour, and surface texture

first applied to the porcelain jar, and later to the woman. We notice, too, the rhythmic relationship between:
> empty, or tenanted by spiders, or honey, or stinking slime

and
> either empty or filled with some corruption.

Thus, we have seen a piece of prose which in its effect, and the complexity of its organization, can easily be compared with many a piece of poetry.

Passages for practice

Students who have worked their way
through the Demonstrations should be
able to go on with confidence
to this section. Some of the practice
passages may, if possible, be discussed
verbally; others should be attempted
in writing, to encourage the greatest
exactness of thought and expression.

1 Fulani Cattle

Contrition twines me like a snake
Each time I come upon the wake
Of your clan,
Undulating along in agony,
Your face a stool for mystery:
What secret hope or knowledge,
Locked in your hump away from man,
Imbues you with courage
So mute and fierce and wan
That, not demurring or kicking,
You go to the house of slaughter?
Can it be in the forging
Of your gnarled and crooked horn
You'd experienced passions far stronger
Than storms which brim up the Niger?
Perhaps the drover's whip no more
On your balding hind and crest
Arouses shocks of ecstasy:
Or likely the drunken journey
From desert, through grass and forest,
To the hungry towns by the sea
Does call at least for rest –
But will you not reveal to me
As true the long knife must prevail,
The patience of even your tail?

2 A Peasant

Iago Prytherch his name, though, be it allowed,
Just an ordinary man of the bald Welsh hills,
Who pens a few sheep in a gap of cloud.
Docking mangels, chipping the green skin
From the yellow bones with a half-witted grin
Of satisfaction, or churning the crude earth
To a stiff sea of clods that glint in the wind –
So are his days spent, his spittled mirth
Rarer than the sun that cracks the cheeks
Of the gaunt sky perhaps once in a week.
And then at night see him fixed in his chair
Motionless, except when he leans to gob in the fire.
There is something frightening in the vacancy of his mind.
His clothes, sour with years of sweat
And animal contact, shock the refined,
But affected, sense with their stark naturalness.
Yet this is your prototype, who, season by season
Against siege of rain and the wind's attrition,
Preserves his stock, an impregnable fortress
Not to be stormed even in death's confusion.
Remember him then, for he, too, is a winner of wars,
Enduring like a tree under the curious stars.

3 A Considerable Speck

A speck that would have been beneath my sight
On any but a paper sheet so white
Set off across what I had written there.
And I had idly poised my pen in air
To stop it with a period of ink
When something strange about it made me think.
This was no dust speck by my breathing blown,
But unmistakably a living mite
With inclinations it could call its own.
It paused as with suspicion of my pen,
And then came racing wildly on again
To where my manuscript was not yet dry;
Then paused again and either drank or smelt –
With loathing, for again it turned to fly.
Plainly with an intelligence I dealt.
It seemed too tiny to have room for feet,
Yet must have had a set of them complete
To express how much it didn't want to die.
It ran with terror and with cunning crept.
It faltered: I could see it hesitate;
Then in the middle of the open sheet
Cower down in desperation to accept
Whatever I accorded it of fate.
I have none of the tenderer-than-thou
Collectivistic regimenting love
With which the modern world is being swept.
But this poor microscopic item now!
Since it was nothing I knew evil of
I let it lie there till I hope it slept.
I have a mind myself and recognize
Mind when I meet with it in any guise.
No one can know how glad I am to find
On any sheet the least display of mind.

4 Waiting (South African Style)

I

At the counter an ordinary girl
with unemphatic features and
a surreptitious novelette
surveys with Stanislav disdain
my verminous existence and consents
with langorous reluctance –
the dumpling nose acquiring chiselled charm
through puckering distaste –
to sell me postage stamps:
she calculates the change on knuckly finger-tips
and wordless toothless-old-man mumbling lips.

II

Was ever office-tea-coloured tea as good as this
or excited such lingering relishing ever?
Railway schedules hoot at me derision
as trains run on their measured rods of time:
but here in this oasis of my impotence
the hours dribble through lacunae in my guts:
Stoic yourself for a few hours more
till the Civil Service serves – without civility:
'Arsenic and Old Lace' andantes through my head.

5 Elegy (on the night before his execution)

My prime of youth is but a frost of cares,
  My feast of joy is but a dish of pain,
My crop of corn is but a field of tares,
  And all my good is but vain hope of gain;
    The day is past, and yet I saw no sun,
    And now I live, and now my life is done.

My tale was heard and yet it was not told,
  My fruit is fallen and yet my leaves are green,
My youth is spent and yet I am not old,
  I saw the world and yet I was not seen;
    My thread is cut and yet it is not spun,
    And now I live, and now my life is done.

I sought my death and found it in my womb,
I looked for life and saw it was a shade,
trod the earth and knew it was my tomb,
  And now I die, and now I was but made;
    My glass is full, and now my glass is run,
    And now I live, and now my life is done.

6 Me and the Animals

I share my kneebones with the gnat,
My joints with ferrets, eyes with rat
Or blind bat, blinking owl, the goat
His golden cloven orb. I mate like a stoat,
Or like the heavy whale, that moves a sea
To make a mother's gross fecundity.

I share lung's action with the snake;
The fish is cold, but vertebrate like me; my steak
Is muscle from a butcher's arm, a butcher's heart
Is some sheep's breast that throbbed; I start
At noise with ears which in a dog
Can hear what I cannot; in water I'm a frog.

I differ most in lacking their content
To be, no more. They're at mercy of the scent,
Of hot, cold, summer, winter, hunger, anger,
Or ritual establishing the herd, smelling out the stranger:
I walk upright, alone, ungoverned, free:
Yet their occasional lust, fear, unease, walk with me
Always. All ways.

7 The Last Word

Creep into thy narrow bed,
Creep, and let no more be said!
Vain thy onset! all stands fast.
Thou thyself must break at last.

Let the long contention cease!
Geese are swans, and swans are geese.
Let them have it how they will!
Thou art tired; best be still.

They out-talk'd thee, hiss'd thee, tore thee?
Better men fared thus before thee;
Fired their ringing shot and pass'd,
Hotly charged – and sank at last.

Charge once more, then, and be dumb!
Let the victors, when they come,
When the forts of folly fall,
Find thy body by the wall!

8 The Hand that Signed the Paper

The hand that signed the paper felled a city;
Five sovereign fingers taxed the breath,
Doubled the globe of dead and halved a country;
These five kings did a king to death.

The mighty hand leads to a sloping shoulder,
The finger joints are cramped with chalk;
A goose's quill has put an end to murder
That put an end to talk.

The hand that signed the treaty bred a fever,
And famine grew, and locusts came;
Great is the hand that holds dominion over
Man by a scribbled name.

The five kings count the dead, but do not soften
The crusted wound nor stroke the brow;
A hand rules pity as a hand rules heaven;
Hands have no tears to flow.

9 The Castle

All through that summer at ease we lay,
And daily from the turret wall
We watched the mowers in the hay
And the enemy half a mile away.
They seemed no threat to us at all.

For what, we thought, had we to fear
With our arms and provender, load on load,
Our towering battlements, tier on tier,
And friendly allies drawing near
On every leafy summer road.

Our gates were strong, our walls were thick,
So smooth and high, no man could win
A foothold there, no clever trick
Could take us, have us dead or quick.
Only a bird could have got in.

What could they offer us for bait?
Our captains were brave and we were true ...
There was a little private gate,
A little wicked wicket gate.
The wizened warder let them through.

Oh then our maze of tunnelled stone
Grew thin and treacherous as air.
The cause was lost without a groan,
The famous citadel overthrown.
And all its secret galleries bare.

How can this shameful tale be told?
I will maintain until my death
We could do nothing, being sold;
Our only enemy was gold,
And we had no arms to fight it with.

10 Off the Campus: Wits

Tree bowered in this quaint romantic way
we look down on the slopes of sunlit turf
and hear the clean-limbed Nordics at their play.

We cower in our green-black primitive retreat
their shouts pursuing us like intermittent surf
peacock-raucous, or wracking like a tom-tom's beat;

So we withdraw from present, place and man
– to green-clad Robin with an iron beak
or Shakespeare lane-leaf – hidden from a swollen Anne.

So here I crouch and nock my venomed arrows
to pierce deaf eardrums waxed by fear
or spy, a Strandloper, these obscene albinos
and from the corner of my eye
catch glimpses of a glinting spear.

NOTES: *Campus* — the ground enclosed by a college or university.
       Wits — a popular abbreviation for Witwatersrand University, Johannesburg.
  Strandloper — (Afrikaans) a beachcomber.

11 The Scholars

Bald heads, forgetful of their sins,
Old, learned, respectable bald heads
Edit and annotate the lines
That young men tossing on their beds
Rhymed out in love's despair
To flatter beauty's ignorant ear.

All shuffle there: all cough in ink;
All wear the carpet with their shoes;
All think what other people think;
All know the man their neighbour knows.
Lord, what would they say
Did their Catullus walk that way?

NOTE: *Catullus* – a first-century Latin poet, notable for his passionate love poems.

12 Drinking

The thirsty Earth soaks up the Rain,
And drinks, and gapes for Drink again.
The Plants suck in the Earth, and are
With constant Drinking fresh and fair.
The Sea itself, which one would think
Should have but little need of Drink,
Twice ten thousand Rivers up,
So fill'd that they o'er-flow the Cup.
The busy Sun (and one would guess
By's drunken fiery Face no less)
Drinks up the Sea, and when he's done,
The Moon and Stars drink up the Sun.
They drink and dance by their own Light,
They drink and revel all the Night.
Nothing in Nature's sober found,
But an eternal Health goes round.
Fill up the Bowl then, fill it high,
Fill all the Glasses there, for why
Should ev'ry Creature Drink but I,
Why, Man of Morals, tell me why?

13 Newsreel

Enter the dream-house, brothers and sisters, leaving
Your debts asleep, your history at the door:
This is the home for heroes, and this loving
Darkness a fur you can afford.

Fish in their tank electrically heated
Nose without envy the glass wall: for them
Clerk, spy, nurse, killer, prince, the great and the defeated,
Move in a mute day-dream.

Bathed in this common source, you gape incurious
At what your active hours have willed –
Sleep-walking on that silver wall, the furious
Sick shapes and pregnant fancies of your world.

There is the mayor opening the oyster season:
A society wedding: the autumn hats look swell:
An old crock's race, and a politician
In fishing-waders to prove that all is well.

Oh, look at the warplanes! Screaming hysteric treble
In the long power-dive, like gannets they fall steep.
But what are they to trouble –
These silver shadows to trouble your watery, womb-deep sleep?

See the big guns, rising, groping, erected
To plant death in your world's soft womb.
Fire-bud, smoke-blossom, iron seed projected –
Are these exotics? They will grow nearer home:

Grow near home – and out of the dream-house stumbling
One night into a strangling air and the flung
Rags of children and thunder of stone niagaras tumbling,
You'll know you slept too long.

14 There I Lie

There where the dim past and future merge
Their nebulous hopes and aspirations
    There I lie.

There where truth and untruth struggle
In endless and bloody combat
    There I lie.

There where time moves forwards and backwards
With not one moment's pause for sighing
    There I lie.

There where the body ages relentlessly
And only the feeble mind can wander back
    There I lie in open-souled amazement.

There where all the opposites arrive
    To plague the inner senses, but do not fuse,
I hold my head; and then contrive
    To stop the constant motion.
My head goes round and round
    But I have not been drinking.
I feel the buoyant waves; I stagger.
    It seems the world has changed her garment:
But it is I who have not crossed the fence,
    So, there I lie.

There where the need for good
And 'The doing good' conflict
    There I lie.

15 Flute-Players

Your flute,
Cut from the thighbone of a mighty bull,
Polished on the bleak hillsides
Scourged by the sun.
Her flute,
Cut from the reed that quivers in the wind
Pierced on the banks of running water
Drunken with moonlight dreams.

In the deeps of evening, play them together
As if to right the sphered canoe
Capsizing by the shores of sky
And deep it
From its doom.
But your plaintive incantations
Do they reach the wind-gods
And the earth-gods and the wood-gods
And the gods of sand?

Your flute
Draws out a note where the ear can catch the tread of a maddened
    bull
Pounding toward the desert
And pounding back
Burnt by thirst and hunger
Felled by fatigue
At the foot of the tree without shadow
Without fruit, without leaves.

Her flute
Is like a reed that bends beneath the weight of a passing bird –
Not a bird trapped by a child
Ruffling its feathers
But a bird lost from the flock
Looking at his reflection in running water
For comfort.

Your flute
And hers –
Longing for their past
In the songs of your grief.

16 Hornbills in Northern Nigeria

As if their great bone-spongey beaks were too heavy,
A party of Grey Hornbills flops overhead
Through the hot, humid air. These are on migration—
('Well, you tell me where,' the zoologist said)—

They emit high, whining, almost gull-like cries,
Seeming, someone says, as if they were mass-produced
Off the production-line of an inferior factory.
But this is not apt. Has it not been deduced

The grotesque Hornbill stems from an ancient race
By the fossil testimony of a small, stony word,
Petrified bone-fragment in alluvial clay?
Look again, you witness a prehistoric bird;

On miocene and pliocene landscapes has gazed
The cold, saurian, humanly eyelashed eye,
Which looks out now over the airfield,
Where forms of camels – not incongruous – stray.

And ceremonial trumpets welcome the guest who comes
By Comet or Viscount, out of the modern century;
The place is not distant from the mediaeval walls,
Nor the satellite-tracking station (Project Mercury).

Here unashamed, anthropomorphic gods send rain;
And dawn, like history, flames a violent birth,
Out of a night with crickets and toads articulate,
For black bodies pushing ground-nuts into the red earth.

17 You Tell me to Sit Quiet

You tell me to sit quiet when robbed of my manhood,
With nowhere to live and nought to call my own,
Now coming, now going, wandering and wanting,
No life in my home save the drone of the beetle!
>Go tell the worker bees,
>True guards of the hive,
>Not to sting the rash hunter
>Who grabs at their combs.

You tell me to sit quiet when robbed of my children,
All offered as spoils to the rich of the land,
To be hungered of body, retarded of mind,
And drained of all spirit of freedom and worth!
>Go tell the mother hen
>Who sits on her brood
>Not to peck at the mongrel
>That sniffs at her young.

You tell me, a poor mother widowed so young,
Bereft of my husband by mine-dust disease,
To let my poor orphans be ravaged by hunger,
For fear of the gendarmes and swart pick-up vans!
>Go tell the mother dove
>Who loves her fledglings
>Not to dare the fleet falcons
>While seeking for food.

You tell me, in spite of the light I've espied –
The light, the one legacy true and abiding –
To let my own kindred remain in the darkness,
Not knowing the glories of learning and living!
>Go tell the proud roosters
>That perch on the trees
>Not to sing loud their praises
>To sunrise at dawn.

You tell me, in spite of the riches of knowledge
Unveiled all around, replenishing the earth,
To live here forever enslaved by the darkness
Of ignorance, abject, and empty of mind!
        Go tell the drooping grass,
        Frost-bitten and pale,
        Not to quicken when roused
        By the warm summer rains.

Tell the winter not to give birth to spring.
Tell the spring not to flower into summer.
Tell the summer not to mellow into autumn.
Tell the morning-star not to herald the day.
        Tell the darkness
        Never to flee
        When smitten at dawn
        By the shafts of the sun.

18 The Snowflakes

The snowflakes sail gently
down from the misty eye of the sky
and fall lightly lightly on the
winter-weary elms. And the branches
winter-stripped and nude, slowly
with the weight of the weightless snow
bow like grief-stricken mourners
as white funeral cloth is slowly
unrolled over deathless earth.
And dead sleep stealthily from the
heater rose and closed my eyes with
the touch of silk cotton on water falling.

Then I dreamed a dream
in my dead sleep. But I dreamed
not of earth dying and elms a vigil
keeping. I dreamed of birds black,
birds flying in my inside, nesting
and hatching on oil palms bearing suns
for fruits and with roots denting the
uprooters' spades. And I dreamed the
uprooters tired and limp, leaning on my roots –
their abandoned roots
and the oil palms gave them each a sun.

But on their palms
they balanced the blinding orbs
and frowned with schisms on their
brows – for the suns reached not
the brightness of gold!

Then I awoke. I awoke
to the silently falling snow
and bent-backed elms bowing and
swaying to the winter wind like
white-robed Moslems salaaming at evening
prayer, and the earth lying inscrutable
like the face of a god in a shrine.

19 Festival

There were six coon teams in Vrededorp that year. Each team tried to outdo the other in uniform, dancing and singing. A team was made up of between twenty and thirty men and boys. Their uniforms were of the brightest and shiniest silk materials. And each team wore a different combination of colours.

My brother, Harry, was a member of the Twentieth Street team. On my first evening back from Krugersdorp, I watched him dress. His shirt was bright red with shining green ruffs and breast pockets. A green handkerchief, tied pirate fashion, covered his head. Over this he wore a red straw hat with three tall green feathers. White gloves covered his hands. His kneebreeches were yellow, with black piping. A broad purple sash circled his waist. The ends hung down below his left knee. He wore red shoes with big shining buckles, and long white stockings that tucked under his breeches. His cheeks were rouged and powdered. Side whiskers and a moustache of burnt cork completed his turnout.

In marching position, each team made a triangle. There were eight guitarists in a line. In front of them walked a line of banjoists. This was slightly shorter than the line of the guitarists. Next came two lines of bone players. Each had an evenly shaped set of bones in each hand. They rattled these, producing a sound like that of castanets. Next came the tambourine players. They completed the orchestra. In front of them were the dancers, in two lines. Each dancer carried a beribboned stick which he twirled while pirouetting about the street. Finally, there was the leader, the apex of the triangle. He was the most elaborately made-up member of the team. His uniform, though of the same colour scheme, was different from that of the rest of the team. He was the brightest in a galaxy of bright peacocks. He did not dance all the time, like the others. But when he did, great artistry invaded the mean streets of Vrededorp, and all my world came out to watch it and be carried away by a *dagga*-smoking, dice-playing, Coloured boy who, for a brief moment in time, carried the gods of grace and beauty in his heart and mind and twinkling feet.

All through those six days, the lucky men, those at work, rushed home at the end of the day, changed quickly into their carnival clothes, and hurried to the meeting-places of the coon teams. There they met the unemployed who had whiled the long day away, waiting for assembly time. The teams fell in. The guitars and banjos struck up. The bones clicked. The tambourines banged and rattled. A whistle blew. The team set off, down the centre of the street. The leader twirled his stick. Those behind him danced.

Thus, they went up one street and down another. And the folk of Vrededorp marched with them. And sometimes, when two teams met, there was a battle of dancing for the right of way. The teams would stop, facing each other. And the two leaders would dance against each other. That was a sight! They whirled and leaped; made intricate patterns with their sticks; danced on their brightly coloured handkerchiefs; on their bellies; on their hands. Right of way went to the victor. The vanquished made a passage and played the victors through. And oh, how the victorious leader danced through that human passage!

20 Civilization

I have not yet defined civilization; but perhaps I have made definition superfluous.

Anyone, I fancy, who has done me the honour of reading so far will by now understand pretty well what I mean. Civilization is a characteristic of societies. In its crudest form it is the characteristic which differentiates what anthropologists call 'advanced' from what they call 'low' or 'backward' societies. So soon as savages begin to apply reason to instinct, so soon as they acquire a rudimentary sense of values – so soon, that is, as they begin to distinguish between ends and means, or between direct means to good and remote – they have taken the first step upward. The first step towards civilization is the correcting of instinct by reason: the second, the deliberate rejection of immediate satisfactions with a view to obtaining subtler. The hungry savage, when he catches a rabbit, eats it there and then, or instinctively takes it home, as a fox might, to be eaten raw by his cubs; the first who, all hungry though he was, took it home and cooked it was on the road to Athens. He was a pioneer, who with equal justice may be described as the first decadent. The fact is significant. Civilization is something artificial and unnatural. Progress and Decadence are interchangeable terms. All who have added to human knowledge and sensibility, and most of those even who have merely increased material comfort, have been hailed by contemporaries capable of profiting by their discoveries as benefactors, and denounced by all whom age, stupidity, or jealousy rendered incapable, as degenerates. It is silly to quarrel about words: let us agree that the habit of cooking one's victuals may with equal propriety be considered a step towards civilization or a falling away from the primitive perfection of the upstanding ape.

From these primary qualities, Reasonableness and a Sense of Values, may spring a host of secondaries: a taste for truth and beauty, tolerance, intellectual honesty, fastidiousness, a sense of humour, good manners, curiosity, a dislike of vulgarity, brutality, and overemphasis, freedom from superstition and prudery, a fearless acceptance of the good things of life. a desire for complete self-expression and for a liberal education, a contempt for utilitarianism and philistinism, in two words – sweetness and light. Not all societies that struggle out of barbarism grasp all or even most of these, and fewer still grasp any of them firmly. That is why we find a considerable number of civilized societies and very few highly civilized, for only by grasping a good handful of civilized qualities and holding them tight does a society become that.

But can an entity so vague as a society be said to have or to hold qualities so subtle? Only in the vaguest sense. Societies express themselves in certain more or less permanent and more or less legible forms which become for anthropologists and historians monuments of their civility. They express themselves in manners, customs and conventions, in laws and in social and economic organization, above all, in the literature, science and art they have appreciated and encouraged: less surely they tell us something about themselves through the literature, science and art, which they may or may not have appreciated, but which was created by artists and thinkers whom they produced. All these taken together may be reckoned – none too confidently – to compose a legible symbol of a prevailing attitude to life. And it is this attitude, made manifest in these more or less public and permanent forms, which we call civilization.

21 Age and Youth

'Sit down, sit down,' the old man said, almost as if he grudged the younger the privilege of seeing all this for the first time. 'Let me see, you want an interview. Do you understand, young man, that you are the first news-hound I've allowed in here since ... Oh! my God, since when? It must have been after the wedding of my eldest granddaughter, fifteen years ago. But you fellows keep on hounding a man, hounding a man ...'

He was silent and the young newspaperman could not decide whether he was remembering the wedding, or what, and himself kept quiet, so that the silence settled again and the very house seemed to doze.

'And so he is dead,' the old man said, and the boy knew that somehow the man had left the other memories behind and was talking about the interview. 'That's what you want to ask me about, isn't it? Well listen, boy, you are lucky, because somehow you reminded me of another young man of your age, only he was your age sixty years ago and more. I like you, boy, otherwise I might never have opened my mouth to the papers again. And now he is dead. It becomes increasingly lonely and cold the longer you stay. All your friends gone. On your own. Your wife gone and your children gone. Your grandchildren too full of life to be bothered.'

The old man had a disconcerting habit of hopping from one thing to another without notice and then hopping back again. But somehow his vision was so powerful that he carried the boy with him and together they moved into the past, the one realistically, the other with his imagination. A small bird came and alighted on the window and inquisitively nodded its head up and down, eavesdropping, and then perhaps felt something in the air and with a reproving twitter flew off for merrier pastimes.

'He and I grew up together in the same village. I was a bit older, perhaps three months. Their house was the nearest to ours and was about three hundred yards away. Between us lay a green sea of *matoke* leaves standing oily in the haze of the sun, nudging their way heavenwards. And then a wind would sweep through them and their murmur would seem to fill the sky. When the rain fell, the chorus from those *matoke* plants was like nothing I can describe. You would feel as if life itself were spattering against and into a womb. So must the first people have thought. I am bothering you?'

Before even the boy could answer, while he was still searching for the words to tell the man that all this meant something to him, like a man who has been away a long time from home and suddenly returns in the moonlight, the old man went on.

'You town boys, what do you know? Have you uncovered the *empumumpu*, that heart-like object growing at the end of a stalk which itself is at the end of the bunch of *matoke*? And this *empumumpu* was made up of layer after layer of itself which you went on pulling off until the core lay gleaming and naked and infant-brown in your hands. And you smelled it. And it smelled like fecundity. The *matoke* garden was more than a garden of food, it was our mother.'

22 This is Experience Speaking

THE INMATES OF MY ROOM

Should I blow or should I not blow my own trumpet? That is the question. It is very unfortunate, but it still remains a fact that the person who blows my trumpet has very unceremoniously left me. Not because he was not sufficiently paid but rather because he could not develop sufficiently strong and projecting cheers to make my trumpet heard amidst the din and bustle of Accra City life. And now, in his absence, I must willy-nilly sound this trumpet however faintly.

By way of introducing the first note, I am a man who always faces facts squarely and is frank even to the extent of being imprudent. I am very short when it pays to be short and I am very tall when it is useful to be tall. 'All weather' is my nickname. I am an intricately complex mixture of all that it pays to be. I am a Bachelor of Arts (B.A.), first class honours in ancient and modern Palmwinology; a master of all drinkables except coal-tar, cascara sagrada and turpentine; a fellow of the Royal Institute of Alcohol; and head of the Faculty of Immunity against Intoxication in the International University of Sparkling Bubbles. I am a man with green blood in my veins and with a more fertile brain than Erasmus. In a word therefore, I am a very important person who is now soliloquizing, with a mind in a cloudy puzzlement, to find out why the Government did not make it possible for me to drive in any of the luxuriously modelled and fashioned cars provided for the VIPs during the celebration of our Independence.

I stay at Accra New Town, in a house where lizards and bats and mice enjoy such first class but highly unharnessed democratic freedom that they freely and easily and impudently spit at and excrete on me, and even go to the sad extent of at times sharing my bed with me. I go out and come home to meet them, carelessly relaxing in my bed, in a bossing attitude. Poor me, how dare I question them? It is just inviting them to multiply their trespasses. What is worse, our desires never harmonize; they are always at loggerheads, always conflicting and always quarrelling.

When I feel like taking my siesta, they feel like having sports. If they would be kind enough to allow me to lie on my back quietly, as an I-cannot-help-it spectator, whilst they do the high jumping and the running and the pole vaulting on the field beneath which I sleep, I wouldn't mind because that would mean training me to be more tolerant. But the pity of it all is, they don't. Sometimes the high jumpers miss and the pole falls on me. At other times too, they themselves lose their equilibrium and fall heavily on me – thus bruising me with their weight and polluting me with their pungent smell. And of course, when such unhappy cases occur, I, the poor victim, have to run to the doctor to cure my bruises and see the ever-ready-to-squeeze-out-money storekeepers for some Milton to wash off their acrid smell. All this is a big agent of erosion on my economic resources.

At times too, when there are no sports, Miss Sun, the residential breadmaker, bakes her bread and, the oven being perpendicularly above my head, I am often more baked than the bread in the hot oven. It is impossible to convince this nagging woman to bake her bread at any other time except twelve o'clock ...

23 Electioneering

Yes, the women had come to the campaign meeting of Uncle Taiwo. They had come to listen to the man. They had been listening to him now for weeks. Jagua knew these women; astute, sure of themselves and completely independent and powerful. Their votes could easily sway the balance because they voted *en bloc*. Some of them had children studying in England and most of them had boys in the Secondary Schools. To them education was a real issue. They went to the mosque on Fridays and to market on Sundays, if the market-day fell on a Sunday. From dawn to dusk they sat in the squalid market with the drain running through it: a drain that could never drain because the water in it was an arm of the lagoon which was part of the Bight of Benin which was part of the Atlantic and Pacific and Indian Oceans, and these could never be drained. In the middle of the market stood the refuse dump from which the sanitary lorries came to shift the rubbish once a day. Many men in the 'Senior Service' came to this 'cut-price' market to squeeze away a few odd pennies from the grasping hands of the big Department Stores. They bought tea and towels, sugar and coca cola, coffee, milk and peanuts from these women who could undersell anyone else because they bought wholesale from shady sources and were content with little or no profit. In many ways these women reminded Jagua of the Merchant Princesses of Onitsha, but these Lagos women did not seem to have quite the staggering sums of money used by the Princesses. Jagua knew that some of them came because they imagined that an election campaign meeting was a carnival, a meeting place for high fashion and love. So they came in their velvet specials: blues and greens, mauve and gold velvets to delight their men who liked them rounded in the hips.

'How many of you can remember your own birthdays?' Jagua asked them. She did not need to be subtle for the language she used was not English. A silence fell at once on the multitude. 'Very few of you. But most of you remember the birthdays of your children. Now is it not a wonderful thing to us Lagos people, that in O.P. 1 an official of that party should be given a wedding anniversary present by his wife? Mark you, I do not say it is a bad thing. I say it is a wonderful thing indeed. But you must all bear with me. The woman who gave her husband this present is a woman like yourself. On the wedding anniversary she called her husband to the seaside. Then this woman of O.P. 1 said to her husband: "My Lord, may we both live happily for ever. Here are the keys of our new building. I built it to mark our wedding anniversary." And she gave him a bunch of keys and pointed to a new house standing on the beach, all six floors of it, and magnificent. A woman. Where did she find the money? A trader, like ourselves!'

'She stole it! ...' came the throaty accusation. Some of the women took down their head ties and threw them on the floor and stamped about, slapping their hips in anger. Jagua spoke into the microphone. 'I am still coming to the end of my story.' They listened, and she went on: 'You see the sort of people you will be voting for, if you vote O.P. 1. You will be voting for people who will build their private houses with your own money. But if you vote for O.P. 2, the party that does the job, you will see that you women will never pay tax. Don't forget that O.P. 2 will educate your children properly. But those rogues in O.P. 1? They will send their children to Oxford and Cambridge, while your children will only go to school in Obanla. No: Obanla is still too good for your children, because – oh! – how can your children find the space to be educated in Lagos schools, if O.P. 1 ever comes into power? No, your children will be sent to the slummy suburbs. These people will open a hundred businesses using the names of their wives. But you? You will continue to sleep on the floor with grass mats while their wives sleep on spring mattresses. You will carry your things to market on your head, and while in the market, you will be bitten by mosquitoes, and your children will be bitten by mosquitoes and develop malaria. And you will console yourselves that you are struggling. Tell me, what are you struggling for? Or are you going to struggle all the time? Now is the time to enjoy! On Saturdays you will kill a small chicken and call your friends. You will shake hips to the *apala* music and deceive yourself that you are happy. But look! The roof of your house leaks when it rains. The pan roofs are cracking with rust. There is no space in the compound where your children can play. The latrine is the open bucket, carried by nightsoil men who are always on strike, so the smell is always there. The bathroom is narrow and slimy and it smells of urine. You call that life!' Jagua was tempted to roar with laughter in the best Uncle Taiwo manner. 'You call that life? Yes, that is the life they have given you and will continue to give you if you return an O.P. 1 government to power.'

24   To the Lighthouse

'Yes, of course, if it's fine to-morrow,' said Mrs Ramsay. 'But you'll have to be up with the lark,' she added.

To her son these words conveyed an extraordinary joy, as if it were settled the expedition were bound to take place, and the wonder to which he had looked forward, for years and years it seemed, was, after a night's darkness and a day's sail, within touch. Since he belonged, even at the age of six, to the great clan which cannot keep this feeling separate from that, but must let future prospects, with their joys and sorrows, cloud what is actually at hand, since to such people even in earliest childhood any turn in the wheel of sensation has the power to crystallize and transfix the moment upon which its gloom or radiance rests, James Ramsay, sitting on the floor cutting out pictures from the illustrated catalogue of the Army and Navy Stores, endowed the picture of a refrigerator as his mother spoke with heavenly bliss. It was fringed with joy. The wheelbarrow, the lawn-mower, the sound of poplar trees, leaves whitening before rain, rooks cawing, brooms knocking, dresses rustling – all these were so coloured and distinguished in his mind that he had already his private code, his secret language, though he appeared the image of stark and uncompromising severity, with his high forehead and his fierce blue eyes, impeccably candid and pure, frowning slightly at the sight of human frailty, so that his mother, watching him guide his scissors neatly round the refrigerator, imagined him all red and ermine on the Bench or directing a stern and momentous enterprise in some crisis of public affairs.

'But,' said his father, stopping in front of the drawing-room window, 'it won't be fine.'

Had there been an axe handy, a poker, or any weapon that would have gashed a hole in his father's breast and killed him, there and then, James would have seized it. Such were the extremes of emotion that Mr Ramsay excited in his children's breasts by his mere presence, standing, as now, lean as a knife, narrow as the blade of one, grinning sarcastically, not only with the pleasure of disillusioning his son and casting ridicule upon his wife, who was ten thousand times better in every way than he was (James thought), but also with some secret conceit at his own accuracy of judgement. What he said was true. It was always true. He was incapable of untruth; never tampered with a fact; never altered a disagreeable word to suit the pleasure or convenience of any mortal being, least of all of his own children, who, sprung from his loins, should be aware from childhood that life is difficult; facts uncompromising; and the passage to that fabled land where our brightest hopes are extinguished, our frail barks founder in darkness (here Mr Ramsay would straighten his back and narrow his little blue eyes upon the horizon), one that needs, above all, courage, truth, and the power to endure.

'But it may be fine – I expect it will be fine,' said Mrs Ramsay, making some little twist of the reddish-brown stocking she was knitting, impatiently. If she finished it to-night, if they did go to the Lighthouse after all, it was to be given to the Lighthouse keeper for his little boy, who was threatened with a tuberculous hip: together with a pile of old magazines, and some tobacco, indeed whatever she could find lying about, not really wanted, but only littering the room, to give those poor fellows who must be bored to death sitting all day with nothing to do but polish the lamp and trim the wick and rake about on their scrap of garden, something to amuse them. For how would you like to be shut up for a whole month at a time, and possibly more in stormy weather, upon a rock the size of a tennis lawn? she would ask; and to have no letters or newspapers, and to see nobody; if you were married, not to see your wife, not to know how your children were – if they were ill, if they had fallen down and broken their legs or arms; to see the same dreary waves breaking week after week, and then a dreadful storm coming, and the windows covered with spray, and birds dashed against the lamp, and the whole place rocking, and not be able to put your nose out of doors for fear of being swept into the sea? How would you like that? she asked, addressing herself particularly to her daughters. So she added, rather differently, one must take them whatever comforts one can.

25 Dilemma

He felt a dull pain inside his heart. He was weary. The country was below him again, but it did not have so much power over him as when he had stood there, a child with his father. The sun was up and he could not see Kerinyaga. And the sacred grove seemed to be no more than ordinary bush clustering around the fig tree. But there was something strange about the tree. It was still huge and there was a firmness about it that would for ever defy time; that indeed seemed to scorn changing weather. And Waiyaki wondered how many people before him had stood there, where he now was, how many had indeed come to pay homage to this tree, the symbol of a people's faith in a mysterious power ruling the universe and the destinies of men ...

Waiyaki stared at the country below him as if he were seeing nothing. Below the calm of the hills were strange stirrings.

What had brought all this trouble? Waiyaki blamed himself. He felt that things had really begun to go wrongly from the time of the great meeting, the time when they all declared him the Teacher. Since then the rifts between the various factions had widened and the attempt by the Kiama to burn people's houses and their threat to Joshua and his followers were all an expression of that widened gulf. Perhaps he should not have resigned from the Kiama, he told himself over and again. What if he had made his stand clear at that meeting? That was now a lost opportunity and he had to reckon with the present. Still he wondered if he had not betrayed the tribe; the tribe he had meant to unite; the tribe he had wanted to save; the people he had wanted to educate; giving them all the benefits of the white man's coming.

For Waiyaki knew that not all the ways of the white man were bad. Even his religion was not essentially bad. Some good, some truth shone through it. But the religion, the faith, needed washing, cleaning away all the dirt, leaving only the eternal. And that eternal that was the truth had to be reconciled to the traditions of the people. A people's traditions could not be swept away overnight. That way lay disintegration. Such a tribe would have no roots, for a people's roots were in their traditions going back to the past, the very beginning, Gikuyu and Mumbi. A religion that took no count of people's way of life, a religion that did not recognize spots of beauty and truths in their way of life, was useless. It would not satisfy. It would not be a living experience, a source of life and vitality. It would only maim a man's soul, making him fanatically cling to whatever promised security, otherwise he would be lost. Perhaps that was what was wrong with Joshua. He had clothed himself with a religion decorated and smeared with everything *white*. He renounced his past and cut himself away from those life-giving traditions of the tribe. And because he had nothing to rest upon, something rich and firm on which to stand and grow, he had to cling with his hands to whatever the missionaries taught him promised future.

26 Democracy

Your Majesties, your Royal Highnesses, your Excellencies, your Graces and Reverences, my Lords, Ladies and Gentlemen, fellow-citizens of all degrees: I am going to talk to you about Democracy objectively: that is, as it exists and as we must all reckon with it equally, no matter what our points of view may be. Suppose I were to talk to you not about Democracy, but about the sea, which is in some respects rather like Democracy! We all have our own views of the sea. Some of us hate it and are never well when we are at it or on it. Others love it, and are never so happy as when they are in it or on it or looking at it. Some of us regard it as Britain's natural realm and surest bulwark: others want a Channel Tunnel. But certain facts about the sea are quite independent of our feelings towards it. If I take it for granted that the sea exists, none of you will contradict me. If I say that the sea is sometimes furiously violent and always uncertain, and that those who are most familiar with it trust it least, you will not immediately shriek out that I do not believe in the sea; that I am an enemy of the sea; that I want to abolish the sea; that I am going to make bathing illegal; that I am out to ruin our carrying trade and lay waste all our seaside resorts and scrap the British Navy. If I tell you that you cannot breathe in the sea, you will not take that as a personal insult and ask me indignantly if I consider you inferior to a fish. Well, you must please be equally sensible when I tell you some hard facts about Democracy. When I tell you that it is sometimes furiously violent and always dangerous and treacherous, and that those who are familiar with it as practical statesmen trust it least, you must not at once denounce me as a paid agent of Benito Mussolini, or declare that I have become a Tory Die-hard in my old age, and accuse me of wanting to take away your votes and make an end of parliament, and the franchise, and free speech, and public meeting, and trial by jury. Still less must you rise in your places and give me three rousing cheers as a champion of medieval monarchy and feudalism. I am quite innocent of any such extravagances. All I mean is that whether we are Democrats or Tories, Catholics or Protestants, Communists or Fascists, we are all face to face with a certain force in the world called Democracy; and we must understand the nature of that force whether we want to fight it or to forward it. Our business is not to deny the perils of Democracy, but to provide against them as far as we can, and then consider whether the risks we cannot provide against are worth taking.

Democracy, as you know it, is seldom more than a long word beginning with a capital letter, which we accept reverently or disparage contemptuously without asking any questions. Now we should never accept anything reverently until we have asked it a great many very searching questions, the first two being What are you? and Where do you live? When I put these questions to Democracy the answer I get is 'My name is Demos; and I live in the British Empire, the United States of America, and wherever the love of liberty burns in the heart of man. You, my friend Shaw, are a unit of Democracy: your name is also Demos: you are a citizen of a great democratic community: you are a potential constituent of the Parliament of Man, the Federation of the World.' At this I usually burst into loud cheers, which do credit to my enthusiastic nature. Tonight, however, I shall do nothing of the sort: I shall say 'Don't talk nonsense. My name is not Demos: it is Bernard Shaw. My address is not the British Empire, nor the United States of America, nor wherever the love of liberty burns in the heart of man: it is at such and such a number in such and such a street in London: and it will be time enough to discuss my seat in the Parliament of Man when that celebrated institution comes into existence. I don't believe your name is Demos: nobody's name is Demos; and all I can make of your address is that you have no address, and are just a tramp – if indeed you exist at all.'

You will notice that I am too polite to call Demos a windbag or a hot air merchant; but I am going to ask you to begin our study of Democracy by considering it first as a big balloon, filled with gas or hot air, and sent up so that you shall be kept looking up at the sky whilst other people are picking your pockets. When the balloon comes down to earth every five years or so you are invited to get into the basket if you can throw out one of the people who are sitting tightly in it; but as you can afford neither the time nor the money, and there are forty millions of you and hardly room for six hundred in the basket, the balloon goes up again with much the same lot in it and leaves you where you were before. I think you will admit that the balloon as an image of Democracy corresponds to the parliamentary facts.

Now let us examine a more poetic conception of Democracy. Abraham Lincoln is represented as standing amid the carnage of the battlefield of Gettysburg, and declaring that all that slaughter of Americans by Americans occurred in order that Democracy, defined as government *of* the people *for* the people *by* the people, should not perish from the earth. Let us pick this famous peroration to pieces and see what there really is inside it. (By the way, Lincoln did not really declaim it on the field of Gettysburg; and the American Civil War was not fought in defence of any such principle, but, on the contrary, to enable one half of the United States to force the other half to be governed as they did not wish to be governed. But never mind that. I mentioned it only to remind you that it seems impossible for statesmen to make speeches about Democracy, or journalists to report them, without obscuring it in a cloud of humbug.)

27 Heresy

It still remains to speak of one of the principal causes which make diversity of opinion advantageous, and will continue to do so until mankind shall have entered a stage of intellectual advancement which at present seems at an incalculable distance. We have hitherto considered only two possibilities: that the received opinion may be false, and some other opinion, consequently, true: or that, the received opinion being true, a conflict with the opposite error is essential to a clear apprehension and deep feeling of its truth. But there is a commoner case than either of these; when the conflicting doctrines, instead of being one true and the other false, share the truth between them; and the nonconforming opinion is needed to supply the remainder of the truth, of which the received doctrine embodies only a part. Popular opinions, on subjects not palpable to sense, are often true, but seldom or never the whole truth. They are a part of the truth; sometimes a greater, sometimes a smaller part, but exaggerated, distorted, and disjointed from the truths by which they ought to be accompanied and limited. Heretical opinions, on the other hand, are generally some of these suppressed and neglected truths, bursting the bonds which kept them down, and either seeking reconciliation with the truth contained in the common opinion, or fronting it as enemies, and setting themselves up, with similar exclusiveness, as the whole truth. The latter case is hitherto the most frequent, as, in the human mind, one-sidedness has always been the rule, and many-sidedness the exception. Hence, even in revolutions of opinion, one part of the truth usually sets while another rises. Even progress, which ought to superadd, for the most part only substitutes, one partial and incomplete truth for another; improvement consisting chiefly in this, that the new fragment of truth is more wanted, more adapted to the needs of the time, than that which it displaces.

Thus, in the eighteenth century, when nearly all the instructed, and all those of the uninstructed who were led by them, were lost in admiration of what is called civilization, and of the marvels of modern science, literature, and philosophy, and while greatly overrating the amount of unlikeness between the men of modern and those of ancient times, indulged the belief that the whole of the difference was in their own favour; with what a salutary shock did the paradoxes of Rousseau explode like bombshells in the midst, dislocating the compact mass of one-sided opinion, and forcing its elements to recombine in a better form and with additional ingredients. Not that the current opinions were on the whole farther from the truth than Rousseau's were; on the contrary, they were nearer to it; they contained more of positive truth, and very much less of error. Nevertheless there lay in Rousseau's doctrine, and has floated down the stream of opinion along with it, a considerable amount of exactly those truths which the popular opinion wanted; and these are the deposit which was left behind when the flood subsided. The superior worth of simplicity of life, the enervating and demoralising effect of the trammels and hypocrisies of artificial society, are ideas which have never been entirely absent from cultivated minds since Rousseau wrote; and they will in time produce their due effect, though at present needing to be asserted as much as ever, and to be asserted by deeds, for words, on this subject, have nearly exhausted their power.

28 The Balloon

It was a noble big balloon, and had wings and fans and all sorts of things, and wasn't like any balloon you see in pictures. It was away out toward the edge of the town, in a vacant lot, corner of Twelfth street; and there was a big crowd around it, making fun of it, and making fun of the man – a lean pale feller with that soft kind of moonlight in his eyes, you know – and they kept saying it wouldn't go. It made him hot to hear them, and he would turn on them and shake his fist and say they was animals and blind, but some day they would find they had stood face to face with one of the men that lifts up nations and makes civilizations, and was too dull to know it; and right here on this spot their own children and grandchildren would build a monument to him that would outlast a thousand years, but his name would outlast the monument. And then the crowd would burst out in a laugh again, and yell at him, and ask him what was his name before he was married, and what he would take to not do it, and what was his sister's cat's grandmother's name, and all the things that a crowd says when they've got hold of a feller that they see they can plague. Well, some things they said *was* funny – yes, and mighty witty too, I ain't denying that – but all the same it warn't fair nor brave, all them people pitching on one, and they so glib and sharp, and him without any gift of talk to answer back with. But, good land! what did he want to sass back for? You see, it couldn't do him no good, and it was just nuts for them. They *had* him, you know. But that was his way. I reckon he couldn't help it; he was made so, I judge. He was a good enough sort of cretur, and hadn't no harm in him, and was just a genius, as the papers said, which wasn't his fault. We can't all be sound: we've got to be the way we're made. As near as I can make out, geniuses think they know it all, and so they won't take people's advice, but always go their own way, which makes everybody forsake them and despise them, and that is perfectly natural. If they was humbler, and listened and tried to learn, it would be better for them.

The part the professor was in was like a boat, and was big and roomy, and had water-tight lockers around the inside to keep all sorts of things in, and a body could sit on them, and make beds on them, too. We went aboard, and there was twenty people there, snooping around and examining, and old Nat Parsons was there, too. The professor kept fussing around getting ready, and the people went ashore, drifting out one at a time, and old Nat he was the last. Of course it wouldn't do to let him go out behind us. We mustn't budge till he was gone, so we could be last ourselves.

But he was gone now, so it was time for us to follow. I heard a big shout, and turned around – the city was dropping from under us like a shot! It made me sick all through, I was so scared. Jim turned grey and couldn't say a word, and Tom didn't say nothing, but looked excited. The city went on dropping down, and down, and down; but we didn't seem to be doing nothing but just hang in the air and stand still. The houses got smaller and smaller, and the city pulled itself together, close and close, and the men and wagons got to looking like ants and bugs crawling around and the streets like threads and cracks; and then it all kind of melted together, and there wasn't any city any more: it was only a big scar on the earth, and it seemed to me a body could see up the river and down the river about a thousand miles, though of course it wasn't so much. By and by the earth was a ball – just a round ball, of a dull colour, with shiny stripes wriggling and winding around over it, which was rivers. The Widder Douglas alway told me the earth was round like a ball, but I never took any stock in a lot of them superstitions o' hers, and of course I paid no attention to that one, because I could see myself that the world was the shape of a plate, and flat. I used to go up on the hill, and take a look around and prove it for myself, because I reckon the best way to get a sure thing on a fact is to go and examine for yourself, and not take anybody's say-so. But I had to give in now that the widder was right. That is, she was right as to the rest of the world, but she warn't right about the part our village is in; that part is the shape of a plate, and flat, I take my oath!

29 Spring Funeral

They decided to bury him in our churchyard at Greymede under the beeches; the widow would have it so, and nothing might be denied her in her state.

It was a magnificent morning in early spring when I watched among the trees to see the procession come down the hill-side. The upper air was woven with the music of the larks, and my whole world thrilled with the conception of summer. The young pale wind-flowers had arisen by the wood-gale, and under the hazels, when perchance the hot sun pushed his way, new little suns dawned, and blazed with real light. There was a certain thrill and quickening everywhere, as a woman must feel when she has conceived. A sallow-tree in a favoured spot looked like a pale gold cloud of summer dawn; nearer it had poised a golden, fairy busby on every twig, and was voiced with a hum of bees, like any sacred golden bush, uttering its gladness in the thrilling murmur of bees, and in warm scent. Birds called and flashed on every hand; they made off exultant with streaming strands of grass, or wisps of fleece, plunging into the dark spaces of the wood, and out again into the blue.

A lad moved across the field from the farm below with a dog trotting behind him – a dog, no, a fussy, black-legged lamb trotting along on its toes, with its tail swinging behind. They were going to the mothers on the common, who moved like little grey clouds among the dark gorse.

I cannot help forgetting, and sharing the spink's triumph, when he flashes past with a fleece from a bramble bush. It will cover the bedded moss, it will weave among the soft red cow-hair beautifully. It is a prize, it is an ecstacy to have captured it at the right moment, and the nest is nearly ready.

Ah, but the thrush is scornful, ringing out his voice from the hedge! He sets his breast against the mud, and models it warm for the turquoise eggs – blue, blue, bluest of eggs, which cluster so close and round against the breast, which round up beneath the breast, nestling content. You should see the bright ecstasy in the eyes of a nestling thrush, because of the rounded caress of the eggs against her breast!

What a hurry the jenny wren makes – hoping I shall not see her dart into the low bush. I have a delight in watching them against their shy little wills. But they have all risen with a rush of wings, and are gone, the birds. The air is brushed with agitation. There is no lark in the sky, not one; the heaven is clear of wings or twinkling dot –

Till the heralds come – till the heralds wave like shadows in the bright air, crying, lamenting, fretting for ever. Rising and falling and circling round and round, the slow-waving pewits cry and complain, and lift their broad wings in sorrow. They stoop suddenly to the ground, the lapwings, then in another throb of anguish and protest, they swing up again, offering a glistening white breast to the sunlight, to deny it in black shadow, then a glisten of green, and all the time crying and crying in despair.

The pheasants are frightened into cover, they run and dart through the hedge. The old cock must fly in his haste, spread himself on his streaming plumes, and sail into the wood's security.

There is a cry in answer to the pewits, echoing louder and stronger the lamentation of the lapwings, a wail which hushes the birds. The men come over the brow of the hill, slowly, with the old squire walking tall and straight in front; six bowed men bearing the coffin on their shoulders, treading heavily and cautiously, under the great weight of the glistening white coffin, six men following behind, ill at ease, waiting their turn for the burden. You can see the red handkerchiefs knotted round their throats, and their shirt-fronts blue and white between the open waistcoats. The coffin is of new unpolished wood, gleaming and glistening in the sunlight; the men who carry it remember all their lives after the smell of new, warm elm-wood.

30 The Blessing of Population

But I prefer to quote now, on this topic, the words of an ingenious young Scotch writer, Mr Robert Buchanan, because he invests with so much imagination and poetry this current idea of the blessed and even divine character which the multiplying of population is supposed in itself to have. 'We move to multiplicity,' says Mr Robert Buchanan. 'If there is one quality which seems God's, and his exclusively, it seems that divine philoprogenitiveness, that passionate love of distribution and expansion into living forms. Every animal added seems a new ecstasy to the Maker; every life added, a new embodiment of his love. He would *swarm* the earth with beings. There are never enough. Life, life, life – faces gleaming, hearts beating, must fill every cranny. Not a corner is suffered to remain empty. The whole earth breeds, and God glories.'

It is a little unjust, perhaps, to attribute to the Divinity exclusively this philoprogenitiveness, which the British Philistine, and the poorer class of Irish, may certainly claim to share with him; yet how inspiriting is here the whole strain of thought! and these beautiful words, too, I carry about with me in the East of London, and often read them there. They are quite in agreement with the popular language one is accustomed to hear about children and large families, which describes children as *sent*. And a line of poetry, which Mr Robert Buchanan throws in presently after the poetical prose I have quoted,

'Tis the old story of the fig-leaf time'

this fine line, too, naturally connects itself, when one is in the East of London, with the idea of God's desire to *swarm* the earth with beings; because the swarming of the earth with beings does indeed, in the East of London, so seem to revive the old story of *the fig-leaf time,* such a number of the people one meets there having hardly a rag to cover them; and the more the swarming goes on, the more it promises to revive this old story. And when the story is perfectly revived, the swarming quite completed, and every cranny choke-full, then, too, no doubt, the faces in the East of London will be gleaming faces, which Mr Robert Buchanan says it is God's desire they should be, and which everyone must perceive they are not at present, but, on the contrary, very miserable.

31 A Storm

A faint burst of lightning quivered all round, as if flashed into a cavern – into a black and secret chamber of the sea, with a floor of foaming crests.

It unveiled for a sinister, fluttering moment a ragged mass of clouds hanging low, the lurch of the long outlines of the ship, the black figures of men caught on the bridge, heads forward, as if petrified in the act of butting. The darkness palpitated down upon all this, and then the real thing came at last.

It was something formidable and swift, like the sudden smashing of a vial of wrath. It seemed to explode all round the ship with an overpowering concussion and a rush of great waters, as if an immense dam had been blown up to windward. In an instant the men lost touch of each other. This is the disintegrating power of a great wind: it isolates one from one's kind. An earthquake, a landslip, an avalanche, overtake a man incidentally, as it were – without passion. A furious gale attacks him like a personal enemy, tries to grasp his limbs, fastens upon his mind, seeks to rout his very spirit out of him.

Jukes was driven away from his commander. He fancied himself whirled a great distance through the air. Everything disappeared – even, for a moment, his power of thinking; but his hand had found one of the rail-stanchions. His distress was by no means alleviated by an inclination to disbelieve the reality of this experience. Though young, he had seen some bad weather, and had never doubted his ability to imagine the worst; but this was so much beyond his powers of fancy that it appeared incompatible with the existence of any ship whatever. He would have been incredulous about himself in the same way, perhaps, had he not been so harassed by the necessity of exerting a wrestling effort against a force trying to tear him away from his hold. Moreover, the conviction of not being utterly destroyed returned to him through the sensations of being half-drowned, bestially shaken, and partly choked.

It seemed to him he remained there precariously alone with the stanchion for a long, long time. The rain poured on him, flowed, drove in sheets. He breathed in gasps; and sometimes the water he swallowed was fresh and sometimes it was salt. For the most part he kept his eyes shut tight, as if suspecting his sight might be destroyed in the immense flurry of the elements. When he ventured to blink hastily, he derived some moral support from the green gleam on the starboard light shining feebly upon the flight of rain and sprays. He was actually looking at it when its ray fell upon the uprearing sea which put it out. He saw the head of the wave topple over, adding the mite of its crash to the tremendous uproar raging around him, and almost at the same instant the stanchion was wrenched away from his embracing arms.

32 Hoeing

Mwangi planted his feet firmly on the ground and lifted the hoe high over his head. He struck the first blow on the too, too soft earth. He struck another and yet another. Thud, thud, thud went the hoe, on and on. He laboured and was never tired. Drops of sweat flowed down his face and their sour taste only added more energy to his stout arms. Lumps of earth were following him as he proceeded farther and farther away from where he had started. He neither looked back nor forwards, lest the length of the field he had to dig should discourage him. All he saw was the place where he had to push in his hoe. He laboured on. He was twenty yards away when Wanjiku woke up and saw him. What was it? She looked up at the sun in the sky and knew it was half past three; the time she started collecting firewood. Was she always sleeping like this? She watched mesmerized as he dug and dug.

Mwangi stopped for breath without looking back. The sweat was too much. His shirt and trousers were glued to his body. He dropped the hoe, took off his clothes and then cut a banana leaf which he tied round his waist. He then picked up the hoe, lifted it and once again resumed his work. As Wanjiku watched, he moved farther and farther away from her. He furiously attacked the ground which was becoming as stubborn as a mule. His black frame dripped wet and as drops of sweat flowed down his whole body, they cut lines in the red dust which had stuck to his skin. The more he turned the ground the madder he grew.

Suddenly, Wanjiku stood up and picked up her hoe. She rushed to his side and wanted to stop him. He barked at her and she gave up. Within a few minutes, he was ahead of her by six feet. He would not rest until the work was over. Was he her husband any more? Certainly. With a force she had never felt before, she went to his right-hand side and started digging. She would dig as long as he dug, and stop when he stopped. If they were to die, they would die together. She soon caught up and fell into step with him.

The earth was softer than she had ever known it to be. They dug and never stopped to see what work they had done. Neither was thinking of the other but only of their field. The sun was, however, faster than they were and the last flickers of light would soon disappear. They went on and on, and neither dared to speak. It was cool now, and a soft breeze blew over them but was not enough to dry away the sweat. In unison, they attacked the enemy who had brought them together. It grew dark but they never thought of going home. They saw the edge of the field and stopped petrified. Only two feet away! They looked at one another and then at the edge. They turned back and could not see where they had started. With smiles they embraced and fell down. There they lay till the following morning when they woke up as if from a dream, completely satisfied of their future life together.

Appendix I (see page vii)

THE PROBLEM OF UNDERSTANDING
POETRY

Surely, they find pleasure in you
    Who read and understand you.
They say your lines
    Which form your body –
Are some sort of music –
    Music which they even claim
    Surpasses that of the town's big orchestra.
They say the rhythms and the rhymes,
    The metres, the imagery and the diction
    They find in you,
Provide better understanding of you
    And your creator's intention
    Or attitude or mood in building you.
Then to conclude their admiration for you,
    When they see all these 'qualities',
    They say you are a success.
You appeal to their taste, to their sense,
    And the genius thus achieves his goal.
But to me what are you?
Do you appeal to me like others?
Sure, I like to see through you
    With an eye of a 'mere' poetry reader,
    But not with that of a critic.
I cannot criticize you no I cannot,
    I can't see the beauty in your diction
    I can't hear the music in you.
Sometimes I try to see
    What images I can form out of
    The imagery you provide
But with less success do I
    See these 'qualities'. The rhymes sure,
    I can see for they are simple
    As learning my ABC.

But why is this? Am I the only one
>   Of all your lovers who finds this trouble?
No, is my answer and so is of many
>   Of my fellow friends, Africans at least.
Beside the different gowns you wear
>   Of the different ages you live,
You sometime speak of places,
>   Places, historical happenings, or
>   Some characteristics of your time
All alien to me and never have my eyes seen
>   Even your description of the furniture
>   Or of the atmosphere around you,
>   Helps to throw me in some bewilderment.
It's all right if I can understand
>   The general idea you convey but
>   When asked to dig more into you,
I sit down lifeless like a stone;
>   And my eyes ramble about the ceiling
>   As if asked to dig the carpenter's
>   Artistry up there.
O! how do I overcome this weakness?
Perhaps I should read more of you.
That I may at the end solve this problem –
The problem of understanding poetry.

M. A. Ibrahim

Appendix II

GLOSSARY and INDEX of Technical terms used in this book.

ALLITERATION repetition of consonant sounds. See page 25

ANTICLIMAX see CLIMAX

APOSTROPHE exclamatory address to a particular person, or personification. (Distinguish from the common mark of punctuation.) See page 75

ASSONANCE repetition of similar vowel sounds. See page 25

ANALOGY illustration of ideas by means of extended parallel circumstances

ANTITHESIS Contrast of ideas, strongly contrasted words or phrases

BALLAD a simple song-like narrative poem, with a regular stanza pattern, usually rhyming *a, b, c, b*

BLANK VERSE a poetic form based on regular ten-syllabled lines, with iambic rhythm but without rhyme. Used predominantly in the plays of Shakespeare. *Note*: this is used only as an Uncountable Noun; it is impossible to speak of *a Blank Verse*.

CALYPSO a poem or song freely improvised, often with a topical or satirical meaning. This type of poem was recently popularized in the West Indies, but has counterparts in other parts of the world. Calypso was a singer mentioned in Homer's *Odyssey*.

CLIMAX the emphatic conclusion of a series of ideas, expressions, or events, occurring in order of increasing importance.

ANTICLIMAX is not the exact opposite of CLIMAX: it usually refers to the effect of disappointment experienced when a passage which seems to be developing towards a Climax takes an unexpected turn, sometimes for a humorous effect.

CONCEIT in its special literary sense (usually referring to the poetry of the seventeenth century) a surprising or extended metaphor or analogy. See page 32

COUPLET a pair of equal lines of poetry, usually of eight or ten syllables, rhyming together, and usually forming part of a longer passage. See page 36

CONNOTATION indicates the references and associations which a word has collected in the course of use in addition to its denotation. Its most frequent usage is in the expression – 'the connotations of this word suggest ...'

DENOTATION the precise and primary meaning of a word

EPIGRAM a short, emphatic, witty saying; often involving antithesis or paradox. Although similar in form to a proverb, it is an individual writer's own creation.

EPITHET a word or expression, usually adjectival, used to attribute qualities

EULOGY praise, usually of a particular person. Used either as a general term (Uncountable), or as a specific piece of writing *e.g.* 'this is a eulogy of ...'. Rarely occurring in the plural.

FIGURATIVE (*adj.*) Expressing not by the direct, primary use of word meaning, but by some indirect device, such as Metaphor, Personification, or Irony.

FREE VERSE a poetical Form with no regular principle of arrangement, whether in line length, rhyme, or stanza pattern. According to T. S. Eliot, 'the most difficult of all verse forms to use well'.

HACKNEYED EXPRESSION literally a 'hack' was an ordinary horse kept for general hire. A 'hack writer' is one who writes for money, without any real literary skill. 'Hackneyed expression' is an attempt at colourful expression which fails because, although the hack writer may not realize it, all his 'clever' expressions have been used too many times already. Examples: the politician who boasts of willingness to 'steer the ship of state', or the student who wishes to 'drink deeply at the fount of knowledge'. See: Dictionary of Cliché (Oxford University Press).

HEAD-WORD a term from modern grammatical analysis: the principal word of a group, on which others are dependent

HUMOUR the characteristic of scenes presented in ways likely to produce laughter or amusement

HYPERBOLE exaggerated expression intended for artistic effect, without any suggestion of untruth or deception. See page 47. Note pronunciation: haiˈpə:bəli

IMAGERY a hackneyed expression, much used in literary appreciation, vaguely connected with description. Best avoided. See page 31

IMPRESSIONISM a method of description giving a typical effect, without the use of much systematic detail

IMPRESSIONISTIC originally used of a type of French painting, early twentieth century

INVECTIVE violent abuse or denunciation

IRONY the use of words or statements in such a way as to convey an implication contrary to that stated literally. See page 33
IRONIC is the normal adjective derived from Irony.
IRONICAL has acquired other connotations, and refers to a situation in which certain contradictions are apparent, *e.g.* 'It was ironical that the millionaire was restricted to a diet of bread and water for the rest of his life.' See page 101

LITERAL (contrast with FIGURATIVE). Expressing the primary or original meaning of words; without any secondary or implied meanings.

LOGIC reasoned argument, proceeding step by step from certain data towards a rational conclusion. See page 20

METAPHOR the descriptive application of qualities from one thing to another, often from the concrete to the abstract. See page 31

METAPHYSICAL literally, Metaphysics is the branch of philosophy concerned with the investigation of basic reality. In its literary connections, following Dr Samuel Johnson, it is applied to the ingeniously metaphorical poetry of the seventeenth century, in which the poet's search for true but unexpected comparisons was 'metaphysical' in spirit.

METRE the basic patterns underlying most kinds of poetic writing; usually described in terms of alternating stressed (–), and unstressed (∪), syllables. The four chief patterns are:

Iambic	∪ —
Trochaic	— ∪
Anapaestic	∪∪ —
Dactyllic	— ∪∪

The individual units of a metrical pattern are referred to as *Feet*. But see page 27

OBJECTIVE *(adj.)* Describing or presenting impartially, without involving, or being influenced by the situations or feelings of the observer. Compare SUBJECTIVE.

'*Objective Correlative*': See page 8; also T. S. Eliot's Essay on *Hamlet* (Selected Essays, London, Faber & Faber, 1951).

PARADOX a witty saying which at first seems contrary to commonsense or reason, though on further thought it is seen to embody an unexpected degree of truth

PATTERN literally, a model, on which many copies can be based. Frequently used to describe types of sentence, or repetitions of words and expressions which produce rhythmic effects.

PERSONIFICATION writing of an abstract thing as though it had human qualities. See page 32

QUATRAIN a four-lined stanza, with alternating rhymes, *a, b, a, b*

REGISTER a self-consistent selection of words, associated with a particular subject, mood, or occasion. See page 12

RHETORICAL QUESTION a question put, not chiefly to elicit an answer, but to make an emphatic statement

RHYME exact correspondence in sound or word-endings, usually at the ends of lines of poetry, usually forming part of a stanza pattern

Double Rhyme is the correspondence of two final syllables. See page 28

Half Rhyme is the correspondence of final consonants with a slight variation of the final vowel. See page 29

Internal Rhyme is a correspondence between the syllable at the end of a line with one contained within the line, usually at the middle

RHYTHM movement distinguished by certain regular features. See page 26. Note the spelling!

SATIRE any form, or piece, of writing which is deliberately and humorously critical in intention

SCIENTIFIC related to the characteristic methods of science, based on Logic and Objectivity

SIMILE   compare METAPHOR. A deliberate comparison, formally introduced by 'as' or 'like'. See page 30

SONNET   a compact poetic form of fourteen lines, usually divided into two contrasted sections. There are two principal rhyming patterns:
Petrachan: *a, b, b, a; a, b, b, a; c, d, e, c, d, e.*
Shakespearean: *a, b, a, b; c, d, c, d; e, f, e, f; g, g.*

STANZA   a group of lines and rhymes which is regularly repeated throughout a poem. There are a number of common types (*e.g.* Ballad, Quatrain), but poets often devize their own.

STYLE   an imprecise, ambiguous word, in the author's opinion best avoided in criticism. See page 22

SUBJECTIVE   (see OBJECTIVE). Observed, or influenced by, the writer's own feelings or situation.

VERSE   another word of various uses. As an Uncountable Noun, it is used as a synonym for Poetry (*e.g.* 'A Book of African Verse'); also to mean metrical writing (*e.g.* 'His later plays were written, not in prose, but in verse). As a Countable Noun, it will be found used synonymously for Stanza, and sometimes to indicate, as in the Bible, a single line, or sentence.

WIT   the humorous effect gained by the unexpected and pointed manipulation of words

Other Works from Longmans

Selected readings in English Literature and Thought
By H. L. B. Moody

This collection of prose and verse is designed to give comprehensive insight into the spirit, diversity and main concerns of English literature. The passages are of sufficient length to indicate the character of the author's work and each provides material for disciplined reading, discussion and further writing by the student. Editorial comment has been deliberately restricted, but topics for discussion arising out of the extracts are suggested to encourage students' own work. A brief biographical note on each author has been included.

The collection is designed for use in General Studies courses and as an introductory course for students of English overseas as well as in the United Kingdom.

Introduction to African Literature
An anthology of critical writing from 'Black Orpheus'
edited by Ulli Beier

This book brings together twenty-seven articles presenting the work of some thirty-five leading writers and, in the first section, accounts of six major African oral traditions.

It is thus a comprehensive survey of African and Afro-American writing and it has the advantage of an anthology in that it does not present this wide-ranging selection from a uniform point of view; it gives insight both into the writers and works concerned and into the viewpoint of the leading critics of African literature.

It has detailed reference notes, notes on the contributors, and an extensive bibliography of critical writing; it will be as valuable to students of African literature, at all levels, as it is stimulating to the general reader.